CU00767647

How to Box to Win
How to Build Muscle
How to Breathe, Stand, Walk, or Run
How to Punch the Bag

A BOOK OF HEALTH AND STRENGTH

BY

TERRY McGOVERN
JAMES J. CORBETT
J. GARDNER SMITH, M. D.
GUS. E. AND ARTHUR R. KEELEY

FULLY ILLUSTRATED

CONTENTS.

HOW TO BOX TO WIN.

HOW TO BUILD MUSCLE.

HOW TO BREATHE, STAND, WALK, OR RUN.

HOW TO PUNCH THE BAG.

HOW TO BOX TO WIN.

By Terry McGovern, Bantam- and Feather-weight
Champion.

FIRST LESSON.

THE RIGHT WAY TO LIVE—HOW, TO BECOME STRONG.

How many of you boys would know what to do if a
larger fellow walked up to you and struck you?

No doubt you are already thinking how you would sail
into him and win. But stop a minute and think it over.
Suppose he should be a fairly good boxer. What earthly
chance would you have against him?

Or even if he knew no more about handling his hands
than you do, and yet happened to be a trifle stronger and
quicker? You would be helpless against him.

Now, this is not right. No boy (or man, for that matter) ought to wantonly seek a fight, or bully a smaller
chap. Still everybody ought to understand how to pro-
tect himself. That is not only a convenience, but a duty.

Governor Roosevelt said in a speech the other day:

" If any of you mothers have a boy who will not fight,

on good provocation, that boy is not worth his salt. He is a coward. Train your boy to use his fighting instincts on the side of righteousness. But punish anything like cruelty. Punish him when he abuses his strength."

Now Governor Roosevelt himself is a fighter from the ground up, as his grateful country has cause to remember, and he knows what he is talking about.

A lot of you will say:

" How can we learn to fight or to box? We are in school or college all day. What time do we get for such things?"

Now that is the very thing I am here to answer. In the first place, you are not in school all day. Only from nine to three. If you study in the evenings, that still leaves you the best hours of the day for exercise. Besides, you must remember you are not training for the prize ring, but simply learning to take care of yourselves and to become proficient at the finest, most useful exercise in the world, an exercise which will give you strength, health, self-confidence, and amusement.

" We can't afford an expensive course of boxing lessons under a skilled instructor," someone else says.

But you can. It shall cost you almost nothing, and I will be your instructor. Such skill as I have is at your service. And as that skill has enabled me to win fifty-five ring battles and rise to the rank of champion bantam-weight boxer of the world, it may also help you.

Moreover, I am not an old fogy, but a boy like yourselve_. I am barely twenty, and have been in the ring ever since I was seventeen.

Here then are some pointers which will enable any schoolboy or newsboy or office boy either, to learn boxing at home. Let me say here that if there is anything about the following lessons that you want made plainer, or any point on boxing about which you are doubtful, write to me, care Rohde & Haskins, 9 Cortlandt Street, New York City, and I shall be glad to explain.

In the first place take care of your general health. No man can neglect that and become a crack boxer. As well expect a race horse to make good time over a plowed field, or Dewey to conquer Manila with a rotten, leaky fleet.

The greatest evils to be avoided are liquor, tobacco, and late hours. I have steered clear of all three, and I owe my success mainly to that fact. Drink especially has ruined more good athletes than has anything else.

It ruins the wind and damages the whole system. So does tobacco.

See that all your habits are regular and good. Keep your digestion in order, eat wholesome food, and be careful in no way to weaken or injure yourself.

"Early to bed and early to rise," too, is a maxim as old as the hills, but as good as gold.

Don't begin to box regularly until you are at least fourteen. Before that the body is not usually strong enough to stand the strain.

I will map out a daily routine for you to start on before I begin giving you regular lessons.

Rise at seven.

Before you begin to dress, lie flat on your back on the floor.   Rise to a sitting posture, with arms folded across

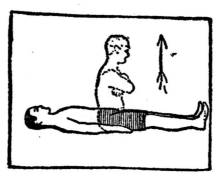

To strengthen the muscles of the back
and abdomen.

the chest, not touching the ground with hands or arms, nor bending the legs.   This will strengthen the muscles of the back and abdomen as well as those of the legs.

Try this five times the first morning.

Increase it by one each morning.

When you can do it more easily, try with the arms held straight above the head instead of across the chest. Bring the arms down to the sides every other time. When you have learned to do this, go through the same motions each morning, holding a half-pound dumb-bell in each hand.

Then stand up, hold the legs rigid, not bending the knees. Stoop over and try to touch the ground in front of you with the tips of your fingers. You will be able to do this in a day or two, even if you fail the first time.

Then throw the arms above the head and bend backward as far as you can. In both the forward and back-

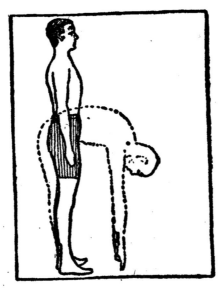

To strengthen back and thigh muscles.

ward motions move slowly, both in the bend and in the recover. Jerkiness is to be avoided.

Do each of these last-named exercises five times the first morning, increasing it by one each day.

Then go through the same movements with the half-pound dumb-bells.

All this should not take you over ten minutes.

Dress and go out for a brisk half-mile walk before breakfast.

You will come in hungry, of course, but eat slowly. Don't bolt your food or gobble it half-chewed. If you do this the stomach will sooner or later revolt. And

To develop shoulders.

when the stomach goes back on a man he is useless as an athlete until it returns to health and duty.

After breakfast (after all meals in fact) take no violent exercise for half an hour. The stomach also demands this, and the stomach must always be obeyed. For if the stomach goes on strike you're a goner till it can be coaxed back to work.

After breakfast do no more exercising until work is over, unless, indeed, you can arrange to walk to and from the schoolhouse or business—not rapidly, but steadily.

When in school put behind you all memory of athletics

The way to walk.

and study or work like a man. For that is the main thing after all, and it is what you're there for. A man who studies faithfully will generally exercise faithfully.

When work is over you can begin exercising again.

After work take a brisk walk of one and one-half or two miles. Keep the head back, chest well out, and mouth closed in walking. Walking is the cheapest, best exercise known, and every prize-fighter now counts it as a regular part of his daily training. It strengthens the leg and back muscles, besides affording general exercise for the whole body.

After you return from this second walk do your hour's gymnastic and boxing work in the way I shall teach you in the following lessons.

After that take a bath. Begin by bathing in lukewarm water, gradually, day after day, getting the water a little colder, but never ice-cold. Don't stay in the bath more than three minutes at most. Two minutes is better. A long soaking weakens one.

When you get out of the tub rub yourself down hard and rapidly with a rough crash towel. As you go on, and begin regular boxing, rub yourself down, after that, with witch-hazel or alcohol. Both are cheap and a little of either goes a long way.

Eat dinner or supper and rest in the evening, for you've had exercise enough for one day.

Go to bed at nine, if you can. No later than 9.30 at any rate.

Sleep in a well-ventilated room.

The only cost of the ensuing lessons will be the purchase of the following articles:

One set of eight-ounce boxing gloves.

Two punching bags (one heavy and one light).

One pair of half-pound dumb-bells.

One elastic " exerciser."

All these things can be bought cheaply, most of them second-hand. Your parents will probably help you buy them. If not club in with some other fellow who also wants to learn boxing, and buy them between you. You can soon do it on the money you now spend on cigarettes, candy, or theater tickets.

And every cent you put into such an investment will return you one thousand per cent. interest in the shape of an accomplishment that may one day save your life and which will certainly make a genuine man of you.

SECOND LESSON.

THE HOME GYMNASIUM—FIRST STEPS IN BOXING.

FIRST of all find some other boy to box with.

He should be somewhere near your own size and build; for it is not good to begin by boxing with a person much larger, heavier, and cleverer, or smaller, weaker, and slower than yourself.

You and your opponent should start about equal. As you learn to box better you can begin to box with men a little more expert than yourself, in order to improve your skill; but don't do it at first.

While I believe that the best fighters are men of the John L. Sullivan type—"natural" fighters who trust to nature rather than to science—yet it is important for an amateur to learn the old rules and motions of regular boxing. Stand up in front of me now, put on your eight-ounce gloves, and I'll give you your first lesson.

Wait a minute, though.

Push back the bed, table, and chairs against the wall and leave as much free space to move about in as possible. You should box, if you can, in a large, empty room.

If you don't care to buy a boxing suit, wear a pair of

old trousers with a belt, rubber-soled slippers or shoes, and an undershirt.

And don't use your teeth to pull on your boxing gloves. Your teeth are good, useful things, but they weren't made for that purpose. Pull on your gloves carefully and don't leave them knocking around the floor after you're through with them. It is such rough usage, and not boxing, that wears out gloves and spoils their shape.

Now, then, come to guard!

Stand with the left foot advanced about fifteen or eighteen inches in front of the right. Don't spoil your balance by holding your feet a yard or so apart, as people do in fancy boxing pictures.

Rest the weight on the ball of the foot. Rest most of it on the left foot in advancing. This not only braces you to resist a blow, but adds force to your own blows, and enables you to throw more strength into back, arms, and shoulders.

The toes of the left foot should be straight in front, not turned out or in. Turn the right foot out at an angle of about 45°, as a rule, though you will soon learn by experience at what angle you can most conveniently hold it. When standing on guard keep the knees unbent and the legs straight. Stand so that your weight can be readily shifted from foot to foot. Practise this until it becomes natural. The right heel should be on line with the left.

Now that disposes of the body below the waist. Before we go higher let me impress on you the absolute need of learning how to use the feet and legs in boxing. They are well-nigh as important as the hands. Work hard to gain a "boxing balance" by constantly shifting the weight from foot to foot, by jumping backward, forward, and sideways, always coming down in position, but

On guard.

with the knees slightly bent to avoid any jar. Do this in the course of your before-breakfast gymnastics, holding a half-pound dumb-bell in each hand; also moving about the floor quickly and striking, guarding, and ducking (still with the dumb-bells) as if you had a real opponent instead of empty air in front of you. Jumping about the room this way, making warlike gyrations with the dumb-bells, is not only first-rate exercise, but quickly teaches you your balance.

Hold the body upright, above the hips, not bending forward or leaning too far back. Keep the chest out and the shoulders back, when on guard. Bend back very slightly, but not enough to injure your balance or to prevent you

Attitude on guard.

from changing position or from hitting with quickness. Hold the right arm partly across the body with the right glove in the center to guard the wind. The glove should be held only about six inches or so from the body. The right glove should usually be held (while at guard) at about the height of the solar plexus. The solar plexus is the nerve center situated just below the point where the ribs begin to diverge into a letter A. It is about here that many a man has been struck, with the effect of losing the bout, or, at the very least, having his wind badly damaged. It is an important point to guard.

The left arm should be extended somewhat further, but not so far that it cannot guard the heart in a close-quarter scrimmage. It is with the left arm, remember,

Left lead for face, showing change of position.

that you do most of your leading, while the right should be reserved for close-quarter work and for guarding.

After you become proficient you can change this guard to suit yourself, but it is well to begin in this way.

Turn the head a little more to the right, not too far, but enough to avoid offering a full face to your opponent's attack.

The first move in boxing (as taught in many good schools) is the straight left lead.

Hit out with your left for my face. Don't haul your arm away back before hitting. If you did that in a real fight I would not only know just what you were about to do, but, while your arm was going so far back, mine would be shooting forward.

Just hit out straight for my face with your left; not stiffly, but letting the shoulder go with the blow, and at the same time not twisting the body out of position, but bending slightly forward to give weight to the blow.

The moment the blow has fairly landed get your arm back to position. Be sure not to lower your right-hand guard when hitting thus with the left. If you do you have both heart and wind exposed.

Next lead with the right for my face in the same manner, avoiding the same mistakes.

Get back on guard. Lead for my face with the left and bring it back to guard. Then lead for my face with the right, bringing that back, too. Repeat this several times. Don't bend the knees when leading for the face.

These two simple blows are among the first principles of boxing, and, easy as they seem, they need a lot of practice.

Now let me show you how to parry those two straight leads.

I will lead at you, and you can parry. When I lead with the left for your face raise your right arm obliquely, keeping the wrist well above the elbows, so that my blow will slant off your arm and not jar it too hard. Be sure to throw the forearm upward and outward with the hands turned out, so as to catch the blow on the fleshy part of the arm.

Raise the arm in time to stop my blow. Catch the

Left lead for face and right guard for it.

blow on the arm, if possible, and not on the glove. In a bare fist encounter you would have no pillow-like glove to trust to.

Now I'll lead with my right for your face. Put up your left arm in the same manner to parry the blow. Now I will lead with left and then right. Parry both in succession, dropping each hand back to position as soon as you have parried with it.

You boys can practice these two blows and parries together now until our next lesson. Let one of you lead while the other parries; then turn about and keep it up until you get it correctly. If you bear in mind what I have said about the position of the body and the mistakes to be avoided, you will find this quite enough for your first lesson.

Get two punching bags for gymnasium work if you can, one heavy, one light. Use the heavy one at first to teach you how to hit. Practice on it each blow as I teach it to you. The lighter bag can be used later to make you quick in leading, ducking, and getting out of the way. Hit out hard and from the shoulder at the bag, not little, half-hearted blows. It won't hit back.

In the next lesson I'll show you some good body blows and how to use your feet.

THIRD LESSON.

HOW TO LEAD AND GET AWAY—BODY BLOWS—COUNTER SWINGS.

By the way, before we begin this second lesson of ours, I want to make one or two suggestions.

In the first place don't imagine for a moment that you can learn each day's lesson thoroughly on the very day you read it.

Boxing, like everything else worth doing, can't be learned in a day. Study these lessons carefully and practice each point with the boy you've chosen as sparring partner.

And that brings me to the subject of that very boy: Don't try to gain the mastery over him or to learn more quickly than he. Be as careful in helping him, in correcting his mistakes, and in all your boxing with him as you would wish him to be to you.

I mean this for both of you alike. You will both learn much more quickly if you help and correct each other.

One more point, while we are drawing on the gloves:

In boxing each other, you and your sparring partner must remember that you are in merely friendly rivalry and are not enemies. Don't "slug," don't try to knock each other down or disfigure each other's faces. All such hard hitting proves nothing, and you have not yet reached the point where you can do it without injury to your boxing.

. Go lightly. Strive to conquer by skill, not by slugging. You are in a friendly bout, not a prize-fight.

Be a gentleman. If you are hit a little harder than usual, keep your temper. No one but a baby gets mad at an accidental hurt. . Remember your opponent is your friend. Treat him as such. You would not knock down an opponent in baseball or try to blacken his eyes. Don't try it, then, in friendly boxing.

So much for my lecture. Now let's stop jabbering and begin jabbing.

Come to guard. Remember the points I gave you in the preceding lesson about position, etc. Now, let's practice the right- and left-hand leads for the face and their parries. Good! You do it a little awkwardly, but you'll soon get the idea. Now for the counters.

I'll lead for your face with my left. Move your head quickly to the right. Not too far. Just far enough to avoid my blow. At the same time lead with your left for my face. Good! You landed square in my mouth, while my blow passed harmlessly over your shoulder. That is the left counter for the face. It's very easy. Don't bend the knees. Be sure to move the head and lead at the same time.

Now for the right counter. I'll lead for your face

again with my left. Move your head again—to the left this time—and lead for my face with your right. Your right arm passes outside of my left and lands on my jaw. A dangerous blow in a fight is that cross counter.

Left counter for face.

Practice both those counters carefully. They've knocked thousands of men out.

Now for the body blows: In these you bend the left knee and throw the body forward to the blow.

Bend the knee and hit out for my wind with your left. Throw the left shoulder into it and hit straight out. Recover. Then, bending the left knee slightly again, hit in the same way with your right hand for my heart.

Those are the two principal body blows.

To guard the blow for the wind, beat aside your opponent's glove with the right forearm, turning down the palm. The right hand being already across the stomach will make this easier.

To guard the blow for the heart, put the left arm partly across your body in a V shape; elbow down, hand at height of throat. Catch the heart blow on your elbow or thereabouts.

Now I'll lead for your face again with my left. Throw your head to the left, so my fist will pass to the right of it,

Right cross counter for jaw.

at the same time bending your left knee and hitting with your right for my heart, as I've just shown. Thus my blow passes you and I run squarely onto your fist.

Let me lead again for your face with my left.

Move your head to the right this time, bending the left knee and leading for my wind with your left.

These are two good body-counters.

Now, if you've done as I suggested about the gymnasium, using the dumb-bells and practicing blows and

Right counter for the heart.

footwork, you will soon catch the next point. Heretofore we have stood perfectly still. But that is just what boxers don't do.

To lead and then to get out of the way before an opponent can return your blow is of the greatest importance. Let us go through all our blows and parries again, only after delivering each blow step back out of reach. Do it quickly, for as soon as your blow lands I am going to hit out at you, and unless you're out of reach in time you are liable to get hit.

Now, then, lead a straight left for my face, then get back out of reach. Now come on again and lead with your right. Judge for yourself when you're within striking distance. You'll make fearful blunders at first in calculating the distance your reach will extend, but you'll soon learn it and it's a necessary thing to know.

And so we go through the different blows; leading,

Left counter for the wind.

getting quickly out of reach, getting back again, delivering your blow and getting out of the way once more.

Practice at this, you two boys, until it becomes natural to you. You can't afford to neglect this.

And now we come to swings. Personally I don't care

much for them.   In all my fifty-five battles I never used a single swing nor saw the especial need of one.

However, others don't agree with me in that view; so I will show you how the thing is done, and let you use it or not, as you choose.

Come to guard.   Drop the right arm to the side. Then bring it around, still extended to almost its full length, in a semicircle far enough away from the body to give it good leverage and to avoid your opponent's shoulder, turning the hand as you do so, so that the thumb will be downward and the back of the hand—at the knuckles, of course—will strike your opponent.   Throw the right shoulder well into the swing.   It must be delivered with speed and accuracy to be at all effective.

I will lead for your face with my left.   Move your head to the left and swing with your right for my jaw.   It is a terrific blow when well struck.   A left-hand swing is managed in the same fashion as a right-hand swing. When I lead for your face with my left, move your head to the right and swing with your left for my jaw.

To guard or block a swing, bring up your arm parallel with the body, so that your wrist is on a level with your ear.   Turn the palm outward, and catch the swing, if you can, on the fleshy part of the forearm.

That's enough for this lesson.   In Lesson IV. we'll try a little ducking, side-stepping, and some more blows and counters.

FOURTH LESSON.

DUCKING—SIDE-STEPPING—IN-FIGHTING—GYM-NASIUM WORK.

For the sake of convenience it might be well for you to cut out one of the pictures that accompany this lesson and paste it up in your room where you can consult it from day to day. I mean the picture of the two chaps who look as though they have five arms apiece. (What a boxer a five-armed man would be!) The five arms on each man represent good and much-used arm defenses for any blow that can be struck. They are worth studying. AA is the right-hand parry for face blows; BB is left-hand parry for the face. C is left-hand guard for a left-hand body blow aimed at the heart or at the wind. D is a right-hand body guard, and E and F are left-hand guards for the body. AA and BB are also good guards for swings for the face, as F and G are good guards for body swings. G is also a good guard for blows aimed at wind or heart.

I have now taught you the primary blows of boxing. All the others are more or less variations of these.

For instance, the celebrated half hook is a short-arm swing delivered at close quarters with the arm crooked at the elbow instead of extended as in a swing, and the hand landing on the thick portion just below the thumb instead of the back of the knuckles.

A jolt is a blow delivered at close quarters, the arm

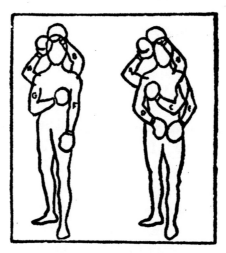

Arm parries for all blows.

being bent and almost rigid and most of the force derived by "throwing your body into the blow."

An uppercut is really a vertical half hook or swing. When an opponent in rushing you or in close-quarters work leaves chest and jaw sufficiently exposed, bring your left arm up in a sort of swing, which should travel upward in a straight line, landing, if possible, under his chin. If you can't land there, hit his face. Throw the shoulder and body into this blow, getting in as much of a swinging motion as you can. If the blow lands squarely and with much force just under the chin it will probably floor him. It is better for fighting than for a friendly bout.

Remember that quickness—both of brain, eye, and muscle—is the very keynote of boxing. Train yourself to observe possible openings, and when you think you see your chance hit like lightning, for in a fraction of a second that chance will probably be gone.

The uppercut is best used, perhaps, when your oppo-

Uppercut.

nent leads with his left, and in doing so chances to throw the head somewhat forward. The uppercut is really a sort of counter. To guard against it throw the head back out of reach or to one side and lead at the same time for his face with your left, or at his heart with your right.

A cross parry is another old, but good, trick. I will lead for your face with my left. Catch my blow in such fashion with your left arm that the left side of your wrist is against the left side of mine. Manage to do this when my arm is extended as nearly as possible to the full and when you are far enough away to avoid the blow by bending back. Throw your left arm sharply to the left, carrying mine before it. This (if I'm far forward and thus shaky in my balance for the moment) will twist my whole body sideways. Take advantage of the moment before I can recover and bring your right glove across to my unprotected jaw. Your right will land on the left side of my face, and the blow is a good one.

Now we will try a little ducking.

The straight duck is most often used. Stand in your usual position. When I lead for your face with either right or left hand, bend your head forward and to the left, moving it in a sort of half circle far enough to let the blow pass over your head. As you do this you can either take a step backward with your right foot, following it with the left, and thus getting out of reach, or you can step in with the left foot and land on heart or wind. In the straight ducking keep your knees rigid and your left arm in such a position that your adversary cannot uppercut you.

Ducking to the side is also useful at times. When I

lead for you with my left turn your left shoulder forward
and to the left, letting the head and the rest of the body
above the waist move naturally with the gesture. Turn
until your shoulders are about at right angles to their

Straight duck, right-hand counter.

former position, at the same time bending the left **knee.**
This will usually take you out of the way of your **oppo-**
nent's blow. You may at the same time lead for his body
with your left hand.

When at close quarters try to get your arms inside
your opponent's and deliver as many blows as you can for
heart, wind, and face before he can retaliate. When, for
instance, he swings or leads straight for your face with
either hand, block his blow and while your glove is still
between his right guard and his face, strike **a short-arm**

blow for whatever portion of his anatomy is nearest you. When you can get both arms at the same time into this enviable position you can have a really delightful time with him. This is known as in-fighting. In such cases don't draw your arms back in order to deliver the blow, but make your shoulders supply the force.

Remember in all sorts of boxing that the whole body must do its share and that the shoulders are an important factor.

A good way to avoid a rush is by " slipping." (Prac-

, In-fighting.

tice this also with dumb-bells in the gymnasium.) When a man rushes you duck to the side and step out with the left foot at right angles to your regular position. Then turning sharply to the left and bringing your right foot around at the same time you can easily fall into position facing your opponent, wherever he may happen to be. All depends on absolute quickness. If you are rapid enough in this maneuver you may even be able to get back at him before he recovers from his futile rush.

Side-stepping is a similar trick. To do this, wait till your opponent leads heavily for your face. Then bring back the left foot alongside of the right, move the right foot quickly to the right, following it with the body and with your left foot, and falling into position so that you can, if possible, get in a blow at your opponent before he recovers his balance.

There is one evil you must avoid. Don't allow yourself to get overtired or to box too long in a single day. As soon as you feel fatigued stop.

At most you must only box about six rounds of two minutes apiece each day. Take a minute's rest between each two rounds.

I also advise you to avoid swings until you become a good enough boxer to decide for yourself whether or not they are of any use. Personally I never use them, as I have said before. I think they leave a man too much exposed. I am always glad when an opponent swings for me, for then I am sure to find he has left some opening that I can take advantage of.

Here is the daily routine I advise:

Go through the morning exercises I described in my first lesson with you, not forgetting to jump, sidestep, etc., with the dumb-bells and to spar with them at an imaginary opponent. Then, after school or business put on your boxing clothes and do the following gymnastic work.

First punch the bag. Punch it two minutes, then rest a minute. Do this four times. Use the heavy bag alone in the beginning. That will teach you hard hitting. Later on use the light bag as well, to teach you fast hitting and footwork. Don't stand up and slug the bags. Go at them as if they were real enemies. Hit; get out of the way; get back with another blow, calculating your distance; and practice on them all the blows I have taught you. .

Then rest while your sparring partner tries his hand at the bag, or else take a turn or two at the elastic " exercise strap." This strap is useful in developing the arms, chest, and shoulders. Stretch it to its full extent, first with both arms stretched far apart in front of you, then behind you; then one arm up and one down, then both over your head; then one before and one behind. Don't overdo this. Three times for each movement is enough for the first day. Increase by one each day.

Then, when you are both rested, begin to box. Don't go over six rounds of two minutes each. Try to help each other, correcting each other's mistakes and going over difficult points again and again until both have mastered them. Before beginning the regular boxing each day, go through the various points I have shown you (blows, counters, footwork, parries, etc.); first one of you acting as teacher and then the other.

If either of you tire stop until rested. If very tired stop for the day.

After the boxing take a bath, dry with a coarse crash towel, rubbing the flesh into a glow; then rub down with alcohol or witch-hazel, and knead the various muscles, suppling them and pinching them gently with the fingers.

Wrestling is also good exercise, if you have any strength left over after your daily gymnasium work. But if you wrestle at all do it in moderation, and avoid straining yourself. Also avoid too much work on horizontal bars, or swinging from rings by the arms.

Too much of such work is liable to make you musclebound and destroy your hitting powers. In all your athletic work employ swift movements; don't loaf or go slowly. Any carthorse can do that. You lose by it.

Skipping the rope may be added to this course of exercise. Skip twenty times the first day, adding five or ten per day till you reach two hundred. Don't skip the rope more often than two hundred times a day at most. If this entire course is too much for you at first, cut it down, increasing it slowly as your strength increases.

In the next lesson I will teach you how to take care of yourself in a street fight, and a trick or two which will make you victorious.

FIFTH LESSON.

No matter how peaceable and well-behaved you may be, the time may come (it may come within the next twenty-four hours) when you will find it necessary to fight.

It is always best to avoid a street fight whenever you can, and to do nothing to bring it on. But if such a fight is forced on you, don't give up as long as you have a particle of life left in you.

If some fellow bigger than yourself attacks you the chances are three to one that you can beat him if only you understand boxing and keep cool.

In the first place, a man who seeks a fight with you on the street may be more or less drunk; in which case he cannot do himself justice and you will find him an easier foe than you expect. Drink makes many men quarrelsome, but at the same time it lessens their fighting powers.

Then again your street fighter is seldom in condition. The man who trains conscientiously and who has a working knowledge of boxing is not the sort of fellow, as a rule, who provokes street fights. It is more often a drink-soaked loafer or tough, who is soft and untrained, or else some wharf workman who, while strong, is slow and doesn't understand how to use his muscles.

Thus far the chances are in your favor.

Another thing that will help you, too, is the grand old American game of " bluff."

For instance, you know in a general way, what sort of man your opponent is. But he has no idea whether you are a pugilist or a consumptive bank clerk.

If you can impress him at the outset with an idea of your superior strength and skill the battle is half won.

When, for example, you see the fight is inevitable, don't wait for him to get into position or attack you.

ALWAYS STRIKE THE FIRST BLOW, and strike hard and skillfully. Aim for the point of the jaw when you can. If not, for some other part of the face. Then, don't let up, but keep right on throwing in blow after blow, without giving him a chance to recover from his surprise.

Don't hit wildly, but with strength and cleverness, as your gymnasium practice with dumb-bells and punching bags will have taught you to do. Make each blow tell, and deliver each blow with full force.

Be careful, though, not to be over-confident or to place yourself where he can retaliate too easily. Remember that a street loafer won't fight fair, but will use every foul tactic to win. There will be no referee there, you know, to disqualify him. Make your superior quickness count in your favor, as well as your boxing skill. While defending yourself carefully, keep attacking him all the time. Give him no chance to attack you or to try any of his unfair methods. Thus steady, quick, aggressive work is often the best way to defend yourself.

The chances are, moreover, that a street tough's defense is far weaker than his attack, and that is in your favor, too, as long as you keep on attacking.

Don't get rattled. If you do your skill and knowledge of boxing will desert you and leave you almost helpless. As long as you remain cool and keep your wits about you you increase your chances of victory tenfold.

Let me say right here (to qualify my remark a little way back about not shirking a fight), if four or five men tackle you at once, don't be ashamed to run for your life. There is no cowardice in this, for it is only in dime novels that one man can thrash a whole gang. In such circumstances escape while you can, for it is not a fair fight, but a brutal, hopeless beating you're running from.

If, however, you are surrounded by such a crowd with no chance for escape, fight to the last gasp, taking the aggressive and using all the quickness and skill you have.

There is something magnificent in the thought of a man battling gallantly and single-handed in a contest he knows to be hopeless. The increased respect of all who know you will compensate for such a defeat.

And now let us get back to the point again. I am more used to fighting than to writing, so I must ask your forgiveness and indulgence for any digressions, as well as for any awkwardly expressed phrases.

In a street fight your opponent will usually try to rush you and knock your head off. His rushes are apt to be

" Slipping."

as clumsy as they are formidable. Here is where side stepping, " slipping," and other forms of getting out of the way come in handy. If you can avoid one of his rushes and before he recovers his balance can land a stiff blow on his jaw or under his ear, you will make an excellent impression on him.

Another point: As I said, the tough is apt to be out of condition. In no place is lack of training so manifest as in the state of the muscles, tissues, etc., covering the stomach.

By following out a gymnastic course you can make the muscles and flesh from chest to waist nearly as hard as iron. But an untrained man has no such protection. Therefore, if you can manage to land a few heavy punches on his wind you may finish him up. A stiff blow on his wind will at least bend him over far enough for you to land your other hand heavily on his jaw. Remember this.

And now, one more point. The man, as I've told you, won't fight fair. If you once get within his grasp it may

Side-stepping.

go hard with you unless you know a trick or two to block him.

He may go even further and kick. If you are sure enough of your ability to cope with him at close quarters jump in at him when he starts to kick and get too close for the kick to land hard.

Or else side-step or get out of the way in some other

Throw across the hip.

fashion, and, if possible, grab his foot or leg before he can bring it back to the ground, and throw him.

Some good tricks at close quarters are as follows:

Suppose for the moment that I am your opponent in a street fight. I hit out for you wildly with my right hand. As I do so seize my right wrist with your left hand, bend your left knee and pull my right arm over your head until your left hand, which holds my wrist, is behind your own neck. At the same time seize my right leg just above the knee with your right hand. Give your body a twist that will bring the back of your shoulders under my waist. Then rise to your full height, swinging my body up, as you go, my stomach resting across your shoulders, my right hand and leg imprisoned by your left and right hands. The impetus, the way my body is balanced, and the momentum of the rise are such that a small man can, in this fashion, lift a man who weighs two hundred. Be sure my body is well balanced (like a see-saw board) across your shoulders, as this lessens the difficulty of lifting me. When an opponent is once up in the air hurl him head downward, or any way you like, to the ground.

Hip fall.

It is needless to say that this maneuver must be executed with lightning quickness. It is far easier than it sounds.

Another: When an opponent leads for your face, counter with the right, sending your right hand beyond his face, so that your arm can encircle his neck. Swing your body around so that your right leg is just in front of his right; catch his right forearm, if possible, with your left hand; then, with a quick motion, bend sharply for-

Back fall.

ward from the waist, using the right hip as a lever, and throw him thus over your hip to the ground.

Again: When he leads with his left, duck, rush in, throw your left arm about his waist, get your left leg beyond his and just behind it, catch him under the chin with your right hand, and, using your left hip as a lever, throw him backward to the ground. This is the hip fall. When a man tries this on you move your left leg sharply fifteen, eighteen inches to the left, planting the left foot firmly there before his left leg can get behind you. This will block the trick.

The back fall is also of use át times. Rush in as be-fore, throwing left arm around opponent's waist, placing your left leg behind his right leg and pressing your right forearm under his chin. Pull his waist toward you with your left arm, and at the same time shove his head and neck violently back with your right arm. If you do this quickly and hard enough he will fall. There are many more such tricks, but these seem to me the more important.

So much for street fighting. In the next lesson we will go back to the gymnasium for some more advanced boxing and calisthenics.

SIXTH LESSON.

THE easiest thing in all boxing is the facility for making mistakes. A blunder persisted in will become so much a habit as to spoil your whole boxing.

For instance, I know a man who might be among our best fighters to-day but for one fault: In his eagerness to get out of the way quickly after delivering a blow he fell into a way of " snapping back." Snapping back is leading for an opponent, and then jerking back the arm before the blow has had a chance to land properly. He has become set in the way of doing this, and it mars many a fine boxer. His best blows thus fall short, simply because he himself will not allow them to land with full force, but instinctively checks them.

Now this often has its rise in a form of timidity—a desire to hit an opponent, yet fearing the other's return blow.

Now this is wrong. Of course you ought to try your best to deliver your blow and then get out of reach, but never do it until your blow is fairly landed.

Moreover, don't be afraid of your opponent.

It is all right for you to parry, duck, and otherwise avoid his blows, but do this only because you want to outpoint him in skill and not because you are afraid of him.

Don't flinch from blows. In fact, there are many

Getting out of reach.

times when it is well to allow your opponent to land on you for the sake of getting a better chance of retaliating with a more skillful or heavier blow.

If you are afraid of the possibility of getting slightly hurt you would better not box at all, for I can tell you now you will never succeed at it.

Outsiders have foolish ideas of the pain a blow will cause. But if you are in good athletic condition the average blow will hurt you no more than would a feather.

The worst it can do is to give you a nosebleed, and a nosebleed is often a good thing for a man. It certainly cannot harm him.

That is where boxing teaches you courage. A man who can stand up unflinchingly before a good boxer, giving and taking blows, will acquire pluck that will help him in other walks of life.

When you have boxed long enough with your sparring partner to become somewhat proficient, begin sparring now and then with some man who is a better boxer than

Forestalling a clinch by an uppercut.

yourself. This will teach you new points and accustom you to guarding against all styles of attack. For each boxer has a style of his own; and after you master the rudiments it will do you good to box with a number of other people beside the one boy whose style you are accustomed to.

As I say, each boxer has his especial style. My own way is to keep attacking my opponent constantly, trying to keep him from forming or executing any plan of attack against me. Aggression is often the best sort of defense. I never swing, but confine myself to straight blows. I keep my feet going constantly, rushing, retreating, side-stepping, etc.

In a fight I generally attack my opponent from the waist up. In other words, I begin hammering at him just above the belt, and work upward toward the face until I find his weakest spot, and then I bang away at that until I get him groggy or prepare him for a blow that will put him to sleep.

When you become a fairly good boxer you can find out by experience what form of guard, attack, etc., is best suited to you. Until then stick to the set rules I have given you, and work faithfully at them and at the gymnasium exercises.

Exercising many hours one day and then no more for a week is worse than useless. Never shirk your daily routine of exercise that I have described. Go through it conscientiously, and in the course of a month or so you will find that you feel uncomfortable if you omit it. Nothing else in life gives a man the self-assurance and the sense of security that is imparted by the fact that he is in splendid physical condition and that he understands how to defend himself in case he gets into an altercation.

When you have worked long enough to make your daily exercise easy for you there is another item that you

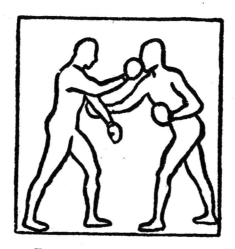

Face counter for a heart blow.

may add, if you care to. During the last half or three-quarters of a mile of your long daily walk you may run. Don't go as fast as you can, but at an easy, fairly rapid pace, and then sprint for the last one hundred yards.

Begin by running a quarter-mile, and gradually increase it by a block a day until you get up to three-quarters of a mile.

A quarter-mile is about five city blocks (running north and south) and three-quarters of a mile is about fifteen such blocks.

Be very careful not to stand or sit in a draught while heated from exercise. Let the gymnasium be well ventilated, but avoid draughts and don't let yourself get cool too suddenly. It is better to endure a little discomfort while cooling off than to risk pneumonia or rheumatism.

Rest on Sunday. Your body needs at least one day a week to recuperate after the week-day training. Six days a week is ample for all exercise.

If you have not time enough in your early morning exercise to use the dumb-bells use them for ten minutes after the punching-bag work is over, during your afternoon exercise.

A man who gets used to sparring rapidly with the punching-bag will usually find he takes naturally to real boxing.

Watch others box. It will improve your style.

In ordinary quick sparring, rest the weight of the body mainly on the ball of the left foot. This not only makes you quicker, but adds to the weight of your blows.

Remember, too, that your brain is an important factor in boxing. Plan out your next move when you can, but let your actions be largely guided by those of your opponent, and be quick to see an opening for a blow.

When you hit, hit out from the shoulder; don't jab weakly at an opponent. Go lightly in a friendly bout, but always hit in such a manner that you could, if you chose to, make the blow tell.

Feinting is a useful trick in boxing. It consists in leading your opponent to think you are going to do one thing when in reality you intend to do another. For instance, start to lead for his face with the left. Up goes his right arm to guard his face. This leaves his heart unprotected and you can land on it with your right. Quickness is, of course, necessary, as your right-hand blow must be landed before he has time to find out that your left-hand blow is not really going as far as his face.

Or again, pretend to strike for the wind with your left. Your opponent may drop his guard to parry the blow. Then suddenly change the direction of your hand and hit his unprotected face.

There are scores of such feints, any of which you can quickly plan out for yourself. Be careful, however, not to be deceived by your opponent's feints.

Now take off the gloves, shake hands with me, and say good-by.

It has been a pleasure to me to give you these lessons, and I know you will obey all my advice faithfully. If you do, I prophesy you will in time become a good boxer and a splendidly developed man.

Don't get discouraged, whatever you do. You can't learn to box in a day any more than you could learn the whole arithmetic in that time. Like all useful things, it requires long, faithful practice.

Practice in that fashion and there is no doubt as to the result.

Let me answer one or two questions from correspond-ents and the bout will be over.

McGOVERN ANSWERS LETTERS.

WILLIAM DAVIS—A boy that is as eager about sparring as you seem to be is pretty sure, sooner or later, to become a good boxer. But eleven is too early an age to begin systematic training. Be careful about diet, exercise, etc., and in three years begin boxing.

C. V. H.—To drive your heel down on an antagonist's instep is good tactics in a street fight where " everything goes," and if you do it hard enough he will probably be helpless. But never, under any consideration, do such a thing in a fair fight or in a friendly bout.

HARRY McCALL—Shaking hands before beginning a bout may not be absolutely necessary, but it is customary and is done as an evidence of friendly feeling.

MICHAEL F.—Hitting below the belt is never allowed. Any point above that may be hit—if you are clever enough.

E. R.—You say you can't control your temper in boxing. In that case either cure yourself of such a wretched trait or box with some man who is strong and clever enough to get the better of you and punish you when you get angry. Whenever you feel yourself getting too much excited or feel that your temper is getting away from you during a bout, stop boxing at once.

P. C. PAUL—I am twenty. I fought first at seventeen. I have been in fifty-five battles. I weigh 115 pounds.

E. H.—Box with him by all means. Even if he defeats you, you will gain practice and experience by the bout. Leave drink alone in future and you will find your health and strength much improved.

L. H. and A. W.—It is better in the beginning to walk rather than to run. Later on you may try running, as advised in Lesson VI. The correct weight of a fourteen-year-old boy depends largely on his height.

A WORKER—You say you are at work from 6 A. M. until 6 P. M. This should not prevent you taking the early morning exercises I advised in Lesson I. You should also be able to walk either to or from work, or, perhaps, both ways, if the distance is not too great. Half an hour during the evening (an hour if it doesn't tire you too much) could easily be spared for the indoor work I suggested. You should go to bed by 9, or 9.30 at the latest.

READER—You say your room is too small for the exercises I advise. Have you no friend who is willing to be your sparring partner and whose house or flat has a room large enough? The apparatus I named will not take up very much space.

G. L.—They can be bought at any sporting-goods

store, or at some second-hand shop, or even at a pawn-broker's.

EDWARD McCOY, Norfolk, Va.—If your health and strength are satisfactory, why should you wish to increase your weight just yet? You are still young, and, by the time you are twenty or twenty-one, you will probably have gained considerably in weight. Use no "medicine" or "drug" to induce flesh. Wholesome food and plenty of it, combined with the course I have prescribed, are all you need.

M. B. LEWIS, Greenwich, Conn.—Thank you for your kind words concerning the good my lessons are doing. Yes, knowledge of wrestling will help you much in a street fight, but a knowledge of boxing is better. Why not combine the two?

F. W. K.—The advice I gave to "A Worker" in this chapter will also be of service to you. The exercises I have described in these lessons will cause the "improved wind, flexibility, shiftiness, and strength" you wish. If you can find no sparring partner, practice on the punching-bag the tricks I have taught you, and go through the rest of the course. You can, however, easily find some-one to box with you.

AN ADMIRER—There is no reason why you should not become a first-rate boxer and all-around athlete, if you follow all the advice given in my lessons.

CESTUS—No. In a street fight your opponent will, three times out of four, lead first with his right hand instead of his left. The knowledge of this should be of help to you. It is the instinct of the average man who does not understand boxing to lead with his right.

J. McG.—A " wrist machine " is excellent for developing strength in wrists and fingers. Holding the arms extended and the fists clenched, and then moving the fist in a circle, or up and down without moving the arm, is also good wrist practice. Holding the arms thus extended and opening the fingers to their widest extent, then closing the fist tight and opening the fingers again and repeating both exercises rapidly one hundred times a day, will strengthen both wrists and fingers. The elastic exerciser or the old-time " chest weights " will strengthen and enlarge the chest. So will boxing.

W. J. FERRICK—The " exerciser " I speak of in my lessons is a simple elastic strap with two handles, such as can be bought at any sporting-goods store.

A. J. E. C.—Avoid drink and tobacco, don't eat starchy foods or pastry. Eat sparingly of sweets, and chew your food carefully.

BELLBOYS—If you cannot get regular hours each day to exercise, regulate your time so as to give you an hour for exercise during some part of the days, as well as taking the early morning exercise advised in Lesson I.

———

And now good-by and good luck to you all.

TERRY McGOVERN.

McGOVERN EXPLAINS HIS KNOCKOUT BLOW.

TERRY McGOVERN's ability to knock out opponents in quick time has been the cause of wonder not alone among followers of pugilism, but among the public in general.

Here is a lad not yet twenty-one years old, weighing 115 pounds, yet he has the punch of a light-weight. When he uses it properly it almost always takes immediate effect. The blow has made McGovern champion.

It was in a great measure responsible for all of his victories. George Dixon couldn't stand it; Pedlar Palmer fell before it; it put Sammy Kelly out; Jack Ward was hastened to dreamland by it; Eddie Santry collapsed after it had spent its force, as have dozens of others.

McGovern has a knack of delivering his knockout blow, and he gets it in without wasting time.

Here is his explanation of his knockout blow:

" Of course if I can finish him in one round I'll do it in a second. That's what I did with Palmer, and we were offered a chance to make $50,000 to let it go for ten rounds for the pictures. I wasn't taking any chances, and let it go when I got him right. The same way with Ward. I got him in the corner and got a chance to let that right short-arm jolt go in, and up she went."

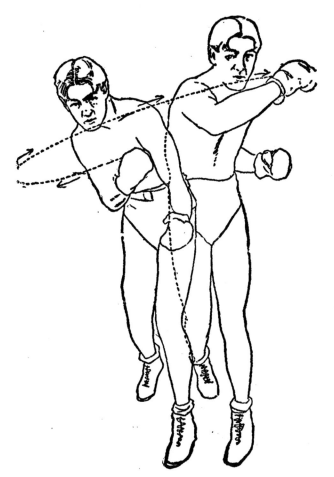

McGovern's great right hook.

"Didn't move any more than eight inches," says Maywood.

"That's right," confirms Terry, "very short."

"What do you do when you are close in that way? come up on the toes to send in the short jolt?"

"Yes," says Terry, "if you stand flat-footed there's no force in it, but coming up on the toes you can get all the body into the short punch, and that does the business. I always do that when I get the chance.

"My hands are as perfect as when I started fighting, I never hurt them. I may bruise the thumb joints a little and get them sore on a fellow's head, but that's all. I always fought straight when I first started. It comes natural to me.'

HOW TO BUILD MUSCLE;

OR,

HOW I MADE MYSELF OVER INTO A NEW MAN.

By James J. Corbett.

CHAPTER I.

GETTING READY—PREPARING THE INNER MAN.

Rise at 7.30 A. M., Exercise, Take Care of Your Food—Retire at
11 P. M., and Do Not Dissipate if You Want to be Strong.

SOME months ago the world at large looked on me
as a back number—a " dead one," wrecked by high living
and altogether unworthy of consideration.

. Since then I fought for twenty-three rounds against
the strongest pugilist on earth, and had strength enough
in me to go any number of rounds more.

To-day people are talking about miracles and telling
of the " dead man " restored to life.

As a matter of fact there was no miracle about it.
What I did was perfectly natural and can be done by any
man.

Now that the fight is over I will tell the secret of my rejuvenation and explain every detail of the process that brought me out of the line of back numbers into the foremost rank of living pugilists.

This I do not tell in a spirit of boastfulness, but in order to help other men whose systems are considered on the wane.

Men foolishly try to coax back health, strength, and nerve by means of injurious medicines or by courses of treatment that only serve to shatter what is left of their constitutions.

I will describe my own regimen in every particular, and I believe any man who follows it will recover strength and general tone as completely as I have done it.

After I lost the championship I went on the road as an actor. Then I opened my saloon in New York.

Now neither of these professions is conducive to perfect physical condition.

My friends believed my days as an athlete were over.

I did not agree with them.

I knew that I could once more place myself where I was before.

So I challenged Jeffries, confident that I would be fit to meet him.

The challenge was sneered at by most people. That

made me all the more determined to recover my old form.

That was last September. Let me describe in a few words my condition at that time:

My muscles lacked their old-time size and hardness.

My liver and stomach were in wretched condition. My nerves left much to be desired.

Now that is no sort of a shape for an athlete to be in. I set about changing it for the better.

I figured out a plan of my own which I followed religiously.

In the first place the human frame is made up of two separate organisms, each distinct, although each is dependent on the other.

There is the outer man—the bones, flesh, and network of muscle. There is also the inner man—the heart, stomach, liver, lungs, and other organs. Then there are the nerves, which form the keynote of the whole outer and inner structure.

I was always quick to find out an opponent's weak points. I was no slower in discovering my own.

I set about first getting my stomach, liver, and nerves into shape. The outer man could wait.

Accordingly, as soon as the Jeffries match was made (September, 1899) I mapped out my plan of campaign and started to work.

Here is a summary of my daily routine during the next

four months. I needed all that time to put liver, stom'
ach, and nerves into proper condition:

DAILY ROUTINE.

For First Four Months.

Rise at 7.30 A. M.
Breakfast at 8.
Rest for one hour.
At 11 walk half a mile to the gymnasium.
Work at gymnasium for one hour.
Walk back home.
Lunch at 2.
Rest until 4.
Walk four miles.
Dine at 8.
Retire at 11.

This, of course, was subject to slight changes.

My gymnastic work was arranged with a special purpose. This was to tone up the system and cause enough
perspiration to force the poisonous humors in my blood
to escape by means of perspiration.

My gymnastic work was all to this end. On reach-
ing the gymnasium I went through the following
exercise:

GYMNASIUM WORK.

Fifteen minutes of postures and motions to strengthen
muscles of liver and stomach.
Fifteen minutes' work with the pulley weights.
Fifteen minutes' steady boxing.
Strip and take a medium shower bath, followed by
rubdown.

The body motions consisted in bending forward until
the fingers touched the ground (the knees rigid) and in
bending back as far as possible (each motion repeated ten
times the first day and twice more each succeeding day).
This is to strengthen the stomach.

Then I would bend to the right, keeping the legs rigid,
and bending as far to the right as possible without losing
my balance, recovering and doing it again, the same number of times as I tried the front and back bending.   These
side motions were for my liver.

The pulley weights (ten pounds to each pulley) were
for these organs also.   I went through the regular pulley
motions, both forward and back.

My boxing was not by rounds nor with a regular sparring partner.   I simply boxed lightly and steadily until
I was tired.   This made me perspire profusely and made
me quite ready for the refreshing shower and rubdown.

To increase perspiration and further expel through the

pores all poisonous germs I hit on a sort of cold-water cure. Midway between breakfast and lunch, as well as midway between lunch and dinner, I drank a quart of cold water (not ice-water, mind you; nor did I gulp it down; but drank it quietly). I found that this quantity of water, drunk between meals, was of great advantage to me in every way. It was good for both liver and stomach and seemed to strengthen my nerves as well.

The water I drank midway between meals, usually after my gymnasium work and after my afternoon walk.

As a special treatment for the nerves I tried a sort of rest cure. I always remained in bed from nine to eleven hours. Even when, at first, I could not sleep all the time I lay still and thought of nothing, and the rest quieted and strengthened my nerves greatly. Of course a strictly temperate life along every line is necessary to the success of this nerve treatment.

To help all the inner man I dieted from the very first. My daily bill of fare was somewhat as follows, (of course varying, but always of the same general nature):

BREAKFAST.

An orange or an apple.
Oatmeal.
A cup of coffee, with sugar and cream.
Two medium boiled eggs.
Dry toast.

I ate a light breakfast, but a heavier lunch.

LUNCHEON.

Steak or chop.
Baked potatoes.
Bread and butter.
Rice pudding.

My evening meal was almost as plain:

DINNER.

Rare roast beef.
Mashed potatoes.
Spinach.
Bread and butter.
Calf's-foot jelly.

I had my meat rather rare. I care little for sweets, so the lack of variety in desserts did not trouble me.

I always arranged my meals so that six hours intervened between them. This allows time for perfect digestion and also gives the stomach a chance to rest.

Just before going to bed I always ate a baked apple or a plate of apple sauce or else a raw apple. This I found excellent for the whole system. Apples are a splendid tonic and medicine if people did but know it.

Such was my daily work for the first four months of my training.

In the next chapter I will tell you how this regimen affected me, as well as my next steps in the process of making a new man of myself.

CHAPTER II.

Keep Your Nerves, Liver, and Stomach in the Best Possible Shape as the First Principle to Work On to Get into Condition.

I HAVE described my methods for putting the " inner man " into shape.

The process was not immediate; indeed, at times I was heartily discouraged; but I persevered, and at last success crowned my work.

Gradually the unstrung nerves grew strong and sound. The tortured liver and the ill-treated stomach responded also to the tender care I was bestowing on them.

By the first of January I felt better than for years before. I was a new man.

When nerves, liver, and stomach go back on a man life seems not worth living. When they are in perfect condition it is hard to be blue or distressed about anything.

In all this time, mind you, I had not been training, but merely getting my system into shape for training, as an artist prepares his canvas for a picture.

I had tried the aforenamed treatment for just one month when I first felt any decided effect. The first result was that I went to sleep almost as soon as my head touched the pillow at night, and that I slept soundly until morning, waking clear-headed and refreshed instead of feeling the dead-beat lassitude of the man whose nerves are on bad terms with him.

The next result followed about a month afterward. My food no longer distressed me. I was healthily hungry for the plain good fare I allowed myself, and felt better after each meal. Dyspepsia symptoms had vanished.

Last of all, the yellow bilious tint left my eyes and skin. My eyes grew clear, my complexion healthy. This I took as an outward sign that my liver had surrendered and was prepared to do its duty once more.

I realized, of course, that unless I continued along the course I had mapped out, these cures would be merely temporary. The routine must be kept up until all the organs were perfectly sound once more.

By the middle of January I was ready to begin active work, and began looking about for a good place to train.

I went—and still go—on the idea that the nerves are an all-important factor in a pugilist's success. Whether a man will prove a hero or a coward depends mainly on the condition of his nerves at the time he is called on to rise to some emergency.

In pursuance of this idea I decided to choose a place where I could be in the open air all the time. There is nothing like fresh air, and lots of it, to tone up the nerves and keep them in perfect condition.

I knew Lakewood was a spot where consumptives

went because the air was such as to allow one to live most of the time out of doors.

This was the place for me, and I went there.

Once there, I settled down to regular training, but of a sort no other pugilist has ever tried.

I have trained for many a big fight, and in the old days I thought I understood how to do it. But I see now I was wrong.

This time I not only had my muscles to strengthen, but my whole system to tone up. I was up against a thoroughly new proposition, and one that required lots of thought.

The average fighter, in training, follows certain cast-iron rules of diet, and works like a plow-horse from morning to night. In order to bring his strength and endurance to the highest pitch he taxes that strength and endurance to the utmost every day, and goes into the ring nervously exhausted, overtrained, and (unconsciously) tired out.

One might just as well try to tune a piano up to concert pitch by banging out noisy marches on it all day.

The piano-tuner keys up each string carefully, testing every move and noting its effect before trying another.

This is what I did at Lakewood.

While training my muscles I also kept in mind the improvement of the inner man.

Fresh air and outdoor life, combined with ten hours' sleep out of the twenty-four, braced up my nerves.

Careful diet and pulley-weight exercises strengthened my stomach.

Horseback exercise—two hours a day—kept my liver in perfect condition.

My daily routine for the first two months was as follows:

FIRST TWO MONTHS.

Rise at 8 A. M.
Breakfast at 8.30.
Walk one mile to gymnasium.
Work there from 10 to 12.
Walk back to cottage.
Lunch at 2.
Loaf about in open air until 4.
Ride horseback from 4 to 6.
Dine at 8.
Retire at 10.

My gymnasium work for the first two months at Lakewood was very light.

It was of a nature to strengthen my muscles slowly, to wake up sleeping muscles and sinews and to gradually tone up the entire body for the harder work that was to come.

For instance, my morning's gymnastic practice was somewhat like this:

GYMNASIUM WORK.

Fifteen minutes' exercise with four-pound dumb-bells.
Twenty minutes with pulley-weights (ten pounds each).
Body motions for stomach and liver
Stand on hands, feet resting against wall.
Punch light bag for five minutes.
Spar lightly for fifteen minutes.
Shower bath and rubdown.

Standing on the hands strengthens the wrist and forearm, besides bringing other muscles into play. I would
only continue it as long as I could do so without discomfort.

I began by punching the light bag for five minutes a
day, increasing this gradually, until in a few weeks I
could keep it up with perfect ease. Then I would punch
it for five "rounds" of three minutes each, with one
minute's rest between times.

I did not try "elbow movements" with the bag, nor
did I butt it with my head or work the "double roll" or
anything of that sort. I do not recommend such motions
for boxers. They are all right for mere exercise, I suppose. But I fancy they tend to injure the reach, to accustom the eye and arm to motions that can be of no use
in sparring or fighting, and to strengthen certain muscles
at the expense of other and more needful ones.

I hit the bag only straight punches and such blows as are used in boxing.

That is the only sensible way for a boxer to use the bag. If you want to be merely a fancy bag-puncher that is another matter.

My sparring at that time was simply to keep me in practice, to strengthen the muscles mildly and to slowly build up my wind.

It was not until later that Gus Ruhlin and I began our heavy boxing.

My diet during these months was almost similar to that of the previous four months. My day's food was somewhat on this order:

BREAKFAST.

Saucer of rhubarb or apple sauce.

Two medium-boiled eggs.

Coffee.

Dry toast.

I would sometimes substitute a rare chop for the eggs, and later I let up on coffee.

Then for the somewhat heavier noonday meal:

LUNCHEON.

Three-quarters of a pound of tender steak, medium rare.

A baked potato.

Bread and butter.

I had my steaks especially prepared. They were thick and from two to three weeks old. This made them easy of digestion, more than usually nutritious, and giving the stomach little work.

DINNER.

Rare roast beef or mutton.
Potatoes, turnips, and spinach.
Bread and butter.
Rice pudding.

Once a week I would eat ice cream for dinner. Occasionally I would also eat jelly instead of rice pudding.

When I went to Lakewood I weighed 196.

This meant I had superfluous flesh which needed changing into muscle. I resolved to take off this flesh and later build up new and better tissue.

The course I followed at Lakewood made me lose three and a half pounds the first week, two and a half the second, and two the third. Thus at the end of three weeks I was down to 188.

While my muscles had not yet increased perceptibly in size I could feel myself stronger.

Then I started in to build up on weight and to further enlarge and strengthen my muscles.

CHAPTER III.

Training You Will Find that the Muscles Harden and the Digestive Organs Become Perfect.

THE work I had done up to this point put me into the condition of a young and perfectly healthy man whose whole body is in absolute health, who is as yet uninjured by dissipation, late hours, or indigestion.

In fact, I think I was, physically, such a man as men were originally intended to be before civilization and its attendant evils marred us.

My nerves were as quiet and firm as those of an ox. My whole digestive system was flawless. My appetite was keen; my sleep natural and refreshing; my muscles those of a strong man in normal condition.

But fighting calls for abnormal strength and endurance. And this is what I now had to produce; taking care, meantime, in no way to injure the system I had so carefully wooed back to health.

In old times, under such circumstances, I should have set to work as follows:

Put myself on some diet which my trainer had found beneficial to other men (whose systems may have thrived on what might have wrecked mine), and worked like a horse all day.

I should have played handball until my strength was exhausted; tossed the heavy medicine ball until my arms ached with the strain; punched the bag for a record, and taken a dozen other forms of exercise that would have strained—or maybe snapped—my newly-acquired health.

All this was not in my line. Certain people may thrive on it, but I believe my course to be by far the better and less perilous.

My plan was to increase my strength and endurance in a perfectly natural way.

I had, ever since I began to train, carried constantly with me a grip machine, consisting of two cylindrical bits of wood, working on an elastic spring. This I held in one hand or the other, all the time, while walking, resting, or riding. I pressed it constantly, until it became a second nature to me to do so, and at last I did so unconsciously. I thus worked the grip machine thousands of times a day without the slightest trouble.

This strengthened the muscles of hands, wrists, and forearm to an incredible extent and without putting me to the least inconvenience.

I began now to increase my gymnasium work. I realized that I was training to fight a man far heavier than I, and I knew how much it jars and tires a man to hit a heavier opponent. To hit such a man hard and frequently takes more out of one than to receive an almost equal number of blows. I studied the thing out and found that, while the hitting of blows like that against an unyielding, massive surface jars the whole body, yet the principal strain comes on the thighs.

The thighs then must be strengthened to withstand the shock, as must the whole body.

But how?

Few people realize that the reason a tired fighter's legs begin to wabble is usually because his thigh muscles are exhausted. Yet it is true.

Here is the plan I adopted to strengthen these:

I procured an eighty-five-pound punching bag.

This bag was of much the same size, shape, and general appearance as a leather mail pouch. I began punching it regularly, every other day.

I used on it the blows I would use in a fight; hitting heavily and only keeping up this work until slightly tired, never allowing myself to become exhausted. I gradually increased the length of time of punching this bag, as my muscles grew more and more accustomed to standing such violent work.

At last I could punch it any number of rounds without fatigue or ache.

But first it was anything but easy. The exercise " caught " me in the legs and thighs. It didn't bother the upper part of my body to any extent. This proved my theory as to the effect on the thighs of heavy hitting.

I kept it up, and found my thighs increased an inch in girth during a single month. Moreover, the old-time jar and fatigue were utterly absent.

Punching the eighty-five-pound bag had another beneficial result. It helped my footwork along and made me cleverer in ducking and side-stepping.

When you punch a bag it naturally comes back at you —and comes back with express-train speed. That's all right when it's a light bag, and an occasional tap on the face from it doesn't matter.

But an eighty-five-pound bag traveling at that rate is a different proposition. It forces you to be quick as lightning keeping out of its way. Thus my work with it served a double purpose.

When I met Jeffries I hit him throughout the fight without once feeling the old-time weariness and wabbly tendency of the legs. Moreover, I kept out of his way, for the most part, just as I had avoided the terrible recoil of the eighty-five-pound bag.

I continued, of course, along the former lines of gymnastic work as well while using this bag.

Next came the question of a sparring partner.

I was, as I have said, to fight a big and powerful man. Hence a man as nearly as possible his weight and general make-up was the best sort of sparring partner for me.

I chose big Gus Ruhlin.

Now Ruhlin is a man of enormous strength, unhurtable, a skilled boxer, tireless, and was in every respect the very man for my purpose.

I paid him one thousand dollars to join me at Lakewood; and I also engaged Leo Pardella, a 190-pound wrestler.

I did not wrestle to excess, or risk a wrench or strain. Merely enough to supple up my muscles and add to my agility and my quickness of eye.

I would box with Ruhlin, not by rounds at first, but until we tired.

And very different bouts they were from my former light sparring. Ruhlin had fought a draw with Jeffries and knew the man's style. Gus and I fought rather than boxed. We used eight-ounce gloves and never got over-excited, but we went in for it for all we were worth. It was great practice for me, as it gave me many lines on Jeff's work. Here and there we would stop a moment, while Ruhlin would explain to me some favorite device of Jeff's, or make some suggestion.

We did not box until worn out; only till a little tired. Then we would stop. My gymnastic work was kept up every other morning. Next I'll tell how I employed the " off " mornings, and what grand benefit I derived from them. Here is an idea of my routine of gymnasium work after I got down to really heavy training. Owing to the careful preliminary steps and the care I still took of myself, it did not even tire me after a while.

GYMNASIUM WORK.

Half an hour with dumb-bells, pulley-weights, and body
postures.
Fifteen minutes with the eighty-five-pound bag.
Fifteen minutes wrestling with Pardella.
Fifteen minutes punching light bag.
Half an hour boxing with Ruhlin.
Bath and rubdown.

Then I would walk back home (one mile) and, after a
short rest on the piazza or anywhere in the open air, eat
some such lunch as this:

LUNCHEON.

Rare steak (half pound to one pound) or
four medium-cooked chops.
Baked potatoes.
Bread and butter.
Saucer of apple sauce.

After lunch I would sit on the piazza or stroll idly
about the streets or cottage grounds until about four, and
would then take my daily two-hours' horseback ride.

On all afternoons this was my programme. But the
gymnasium work I did only every other day.

CHAPTER IV.

FRESH AIR A MUSCLE-BUILDER.

Fresh Air and Cold Water Will Build Up a Man Better than Any Medicine.

I AM something of a crank on the subject of fresh air.

I believe fresh air and plenty of pure, cold water will build a man up better than all the medicines on earth.

Except for the two hours every other day spent in my well-ventilated gymnasium, and the time I spent at meals, I was in the open air from 8 A. M. until 10 P. M. every day for the last four months of my training. I slept always in a room whose windows were wide open.

All this was of inestimable benefit to my nerves, making them like iron, and hence toned up my entire system.

On " off " mornings I would leave my cottage at about 9.30 and would start off with my collie, Saddie, at my heels for a tramp.

The roads about Lakewood are pretty good, and the land lies level, permitting cross-country running.

I chose a different route every day.

I would begin the morning exercise by walking a mile at an ordinary gait at first, then hitting up the pace to a brisk stride.

At the end of a mile I would sprint at top speed for a furlong, then slow down to a second mile of quick walking, followed by another 220-yard sprint.

Then I would follow the next mile of walking by a quarter-mile jog trot, covering the quarter in about 58 or 60 seconds.

I would keep up these pedestrian feats for about six miles and would then turn back, returning home in the same fashion, covering twelve miles in all.

Of course, I did not take such long walks at first, but started with four miles, increasing by half a mile a day, until I could do the entire twelve miles without turning a hair.

While thus exercising I kept the lips closed, breathing through the nose, holding the shoulders well back and the chest out, though not unnaturally so.

I ran on the ball of the foot. Never flat-footed. This strengthened the whole leg, from ankle to thigh.

Occasionally I varied road work by cross-country running, taking a bee-line through wood and meadow, vaulting the fences in my way.

I would return from my walk, take a bath and rub-down, and be ready to eat everything in sight.

The routine for my " off days " was as follows:

ROUTINE FOR OFF DAYS.

Rise at 8.

Breakfast at 8.30.

Take the road at 9.30.

Walk one mile.

Sprint one furlong.

Walk one mile.

Jog one quarter-mile.

And so on for twelve miles.

Bath and rubdown.

Rest on piazza until 2.

Lunch.

Loaf about (out of doors) till 4.

Ride horseback till 6.

Dine at 8.

Retire at 10.

By taking one morning for gymnastic work and the next for outdoor exercise, I varied the monotony of training which tells so heavily on a man of nervous temperament, besides avoiding all strain on my nerves by sticking too constantly to any one pursuit.

Another strong factor in my success was the fact that, outside of work hours, I lived my usual home life. The average pugilist, on going into training, leaves home and home comforts, and takes up quarters with a crowd of men who may or may not be congenial to him. He has no home life; he is separated from friends and kindred.

With me it was different.

I rented a pleasant cottage in the residence part of Lakewood, furnished it to suit my own tastes, and lived there with my wife and our own servants throughout my training course. I had friends run down to visit us, and in every way kept up the pleasant home life that my domestic tastes render so delightful to me.

I consider this a prominent item in the success of my training.

By the first of April I felt fit to put up the battle of my life.

My "inner man" was sound as a bell. My nerves had never in all my life been in such magnificent condition. My muscles were flexible steel. I was agile, powerful; capable of greater endurance than ever before.

Yet my training had been ridiculously light, compared to that taken by the average pugilist.

I now began cautiously to test my endurance and strength.

For instance, I twice boxed twenty-five-round bouts with Gus Ruhlin. And they were no play bouts, either. We both went at it for all we were worth. Between rounds we had no one to fan us, spurt water over us, or perform any of the kind offices of second. We stood up, too, in the interval of rest.

Neither bout exhausted me. And that strikes me as about the best possible proof of my great condition. If you had ever stood before Ruhlin for twenty-five rounds you would understand what I mean.

Heretofore I have wasted much time and energy in worrying over the prospects of a fight—in making and unmaking plans of action. Now, that was pure nervousness.

Also, in all my other fights I went to the ringside nervous from head to foot. Not in the very least frightened, you understand, but terribly nervous as to the result—even as a Wall Street man is when he awaits the whir of the ticker which is to tell him whether he is a millionaire or a pauper. Such nervousness weakens a fighter.

This time it was all different.

I laid out a plan of action as coolly and dispassionately as if for some other person. That once done, I gave the matter no further worry.

When the day of the fight came I can truthfully say I felt no more nervousness than if I were going into a friendly boxing match. I was perfectly cool, and not a tremor or qualm of nervousness troubled me.

Moreover, I found I could endure with perfect ease blows and rushes that would in the old time have worn me out. The blows Jeffries planted on my stomach (thinking it, no doubt, my weak point) did not bother me in the very least. The stomach I had so tenderly nursed back to health stood by me nobly in my hour of need.

The blows I struck never jarred me as of yore. My thighs and legs were strong enough to avert that.

As for endurance, everyone knows I was perfectly fresh and strong at the beginning of the twenty-third round. I was strong enough to have gone on for any number of additional rounds.

If I were asked to what I owe my rehabilitation and my creditable showing, I should say:

First and foremost, to regular, normal living.

Second, to fresh air (the athlete's best assistant).

Third, to absence of worry.

Fourth, to my moderate, easy, long training.

Any run-down, exhausted, or over-worked man can rejuvenate himself and restore his entire system as easily as I did. From a hygienic point of view it pays better than any other investment on earth.

Now, I have talked enough about myself, and I am going to venture upon the rôle of physical instructor.

Will you take lessons from me?

It so, I will devote an article in the next chapter telling men who lead a sedentary or dissipated life how to make over their systems as good as new and how to become athletes without in the very least neglecting their business or profession.

In the sixth chapter I will tell women how to build up

constitutions shattered by the hard work of a New York society season or by overwork in factory, store, or office. I will also teach them how to improve the figure, to strengthen flaccid muscles, and to renew health, complexion, and vivacity.

CHAPTER V

How to Make Over Your System as Good as New, and How to
Become an Athlete Without Neglecting Business.

" How many men, do you suppose, are in perfect
health?

" Scarcely one-half," perhaps you say. I tell you not
one in ten.

These men are not actually ill, for the most part. But
few of them could run three blocks without puffing; seldom they awake full of energy and free from stupidity or
lassitude.

Let them take violent exercise one day, and the next
morning they will be stiff and sore from head to foot.
Let them be subjected to some sudden excitement and
they will flush or turn pale or tremble.

Do you call all that being in good health?

I don't.

Muscles, nerves, and internal apparatus are out of gear
to produce such results.

Are you content to remain like that? If so, don't read
this lesson. It isn't intended for you.

Or rather do you say:

"I'd like to be in sound physical shape; but I don't know how to accomplish it. I'm too busy to spare time on athletics. I'm too poor to join a gymnasium; but if you'll teach me how to get well and strong, I'll follow your instructions, even at the cost of a certain amount of inconvenience."

If you belong to this latter class of men, it is to you I'm writing. And when you're in good shape once more you can say, if you care to:

"Jim Corbett was my physical instructor."

I'll stand for it.

In the first place, I'll give you no advice that I myself have not tried and found to be good.

I am supposing you are a business or professional man, or perhaps a working man.

I was a bank clerk for years, and I know how hard it is for a man leading such a sedentary life to follow athletics, but it isn't impossible.

I did it. So can you.

Let me map out your daily programme.

We will suppose you have to reach your place of business by nine. (If earlier or later, arrange your programme in the desired hours, keeping the same ratio I shall suggest for the nine-o'clock basis.)

Get up at seven. Strip and take up a pair of one or two-pound dumb-bells (no heavier). Practice with them, using the regular simple motions as described in any manual or as the man at the sporting store where you buy the bells will show you. Keep this up steadily and briskly for fifteen minutes.

Then stand with legs rigid, bending over forward and touching the floor with the tips of your fingers. You may not be able to do this just at first; but you can very soon. Do it five times the first morning, increasing by two each day till you get to twenty-five. Then keep it at that.

Bend slowly backward as far as you can without straining yourself; then return slowly to an upright posture. Do this the same number of times as the forward motion.

Next lie flat on your back on the floor, your arms crossed on your chest. Rise to a sitting posture without bending the legs or uncrossing the arms. Then sink back, and repeat as often as the bending forward and back motions.

These moves strengthen the whole body, notably the stomach, back, and legs.

Then stand up and draw, slowly, a long breath, until the lungs are full. Let out the breath just as slowly. Repeat this ten times. The lungs are thus expanded, cleared of poisonous gases, and strengthened.

Now jump into a cold bath. Have the bath prepared the night before, throwing into it two or three handfuls of sea salt and allowing it to soak all night. This sea salt can be bought cheap at any drug store. Jump into the bath, wash as quickly as you can, and jump out again.

Then rub yourself dry with a rough bath towel and dress. After bathing drink a glass of water.

If you have any heart trouble, let the bath be slightly warmed; otherwise not.

By the time you reach the dining room you will probably be very hungry.

But eat lightly. We Americans eat too much anyway. A heavy meat breakfast is almost as bad for one as no breakfast at all. It clogs the system, causes lassitude, and overworks the stomach before that organ is toned up for its daily toil.

Let your breakfast be somewhat as follows:

BREAKFAST.

Fruit.
Oatmeal.
Two medium-boiled eggs.
One cup of coffee.
Dry toast.

A man needs less variety at breakfast than at other meals. Substitute hominy or any other cereal for oatmeal, if you like; or tea or coffee. If you can it is a little better to do without either of the latter. At most never drink more than one cup. Don't bolt your food at any meal. We are a race of dyspeptics because we gulp down our food like wild beasts. Take half an hour for both breakfast and lunch and an hour for dinner.

Now start for your office. If you live within a mile or so of your place of business, always walk to and from work. If you live far uptown take the cars part of the way; then, a mile above your office, get out and walk the rest of the way. This walk is necessary. While walking keep erect, chest thrown out, lips closed, breathing through the nose.

Don't loaf along, but walk briskly. This walk gives your lungs plenty of pure, fresh air, and thus acts as a tonic for the whole body. It also strengthens the leg muscles.

If possible go out for lunch. You need the change of air. Don't eat pastry or other indigestible food at this meal. Here is a good lunch diet:

LUNCHEON.

Two chops or a portion of stew or cold meat.
Potatoes.
Spinach.
Pudding or ice-cream.

If your work keeps you indoors all day a lighter lunch will serve. Cut off dessert and one vegetable.

When through work walk at least a mile on your homeward way.

Then, if you can possibly arrange time, take an hour before dinner for gymnastic work. You will feel too tired to do this at first; but force yourself, and it will soon come natural and will be of inestimable benefit.

New York is full of good gymnasiums both for rich and poor. If you cannot afford one of the private gymnasiums, attend one of those belonging to the Y. M. C. A.

There take fifteen minutes' exercise with the pulley-weights, punch the bag for five minutes, get someone, if possible, to box or wrestle with you (not too violently) for ten minutes. If there is a running track there, try a few laps on it. If there is a handball court use it, but in moderation. Never keep on when really exhausted, but stop and rest. If you don't get rested soon, leave off until the next day.

At dinner you may, if you choose, eat more heartily. Here is a pretty good dinner for a man in light training'

DINNER.

Soup.
Boiled, broiled, or baked fish.
Roast beef, mutton, or chicken.
Potatoes, rice, spinach, peas.
Tomato salad.
Ice-cream, jelly, or pudding, and cake.

Take an hour for dinner. Eat slowly. Chew your food well. Steer clear of pastry and fried foods. Never eat a mouthful after you cease to be hungry. Never force yourself to eat more just because the meal is not yet over.

Go to bed between 10 and 11 P. M. When undressed take another cold bath and rub down, jumping into the water and straight out again.

Then, just before getting to bed (after the bath) eat, with a wafer or cracker and a glass of water, a saucer of stewed prunes, rhubarb, or apple sauce.

Sleep in a well-ventilated room with only enough covers to keep you comfortable.

Now for some additional points:

Be sure to drink plenty of cold water (not iced) and be sure it is filtered free of disease germs. The more water you drink the better it will be for you. Water and exercise bring on perspiration, and this draws away the poisons of the blood and renews health.

Keep every function of the body in regular and perfect condition. This is all-important.

Get all the sleep you can. The more nervous a man is the more sleep he needs.

Let up as much as possible on drink and tobacco. If you are accustomed to both and dependent on them, a glass of claret with dinner and a single cigar or a pipe afterward will do you no great harm. Leave cigarettes alone.

Lead a straight, normal life. Try not to worry. Banish blues by exercise and healthy thoughts.

By work and water-drinking force yourself to perspire. No man can be well otherwise.

If you can afford it, brace up the liver by horseback riding. If not, take long tramps.

Bicycling is also good, but too smooth an exercise to shake up the liver to any extent.

Follow every one of the above rules, and (unless you have some serious disease) you will find yourself in time healthy in body, strong in muscle, clear and vigorous in brain.

Don't imagine, however, that any of those results will come in a day, or at all, for that matter, unless you follow the course of training faithfully. Never skip a day, no matter how many other things may demand your time, but always follow the programme I have laid down.

It made me over again.

It will do the same for you.

CHAPTER VI.

HOW WOMEN MAY GROW STRONG AND BEAUTIFUL.

Mild Exercise, Careful Diet, and Simple Rules of Hygiene Prescribed for All Classes of Women.

I AM not a beauty expert nor a specialist. So don't expect too much from me.

But I am a man who has made a long and successful study of health; of the human system, and of the best ways to restore it to perfect condition.

The hints I shall give to women are not those of a physician, but of an ordinary man. Don't disregard them on that account. Give them a trial. I shall advise nothing that can possibly injure you; and if you follow my instructions faithfully I can promise that you will be stronger, healthier, and sounder in every respect.

ADVICE TO WOMEN.

In the first place, the rules of training that benefit men cannot be used in most cases for women.

Let me therefore map out a separate day's programme for women, just as I did for men in the last chapter; and add some beneficial suggestions.

We will suppose you have worn yourself out by late hours, by dancing, by eating incongruous, murderous combinations of food at the wrong time of day, and by lack of exercise.

Or else that you are employed in some office, store, or factory where you get to work early, toil indoors all day in a badly ventilated room, and go home exhausted. Your recreations are often as tiring as your work. Your lunch consists largely of pie or some other form of pastry. Your other meals are bolted in order to get to work or to some place of amusement.

Yet you wonder why you feel badly; why your head aches; why you tire so easily; why your fresh, girlish complexion is growing coarse and muddy.

Men may knock out their stomachs by drink, tobacco, and a dozen other forms of dissipation, but I'll venture to assert that the most dissipated man takes better care of his stomach than the average carefully nurtured woman. Don't laugh at this statement just yet, please.

A man is hungry, we will say. He goes to a restaurant and orders a steak, a chop, or some roast beef. He drinks beer with it, and potatoes are his only vegetable.

WHAT NOT TO EAT.

A woman, on the other hand, will feel hungry while out shopping. She will go to the nearest lunch-room and order fried oysters and ice-cream. Now, isn't that a combination to make the gods weep? Or else, if. not very hungry, a bit of pastry and a glass of soda water suffice her. Going home after lunch she will sit around and eat candy. If she is thirsty while out of doors she stops and buys a glass of ice-cream soda—on an empty stomach, too!

Then she wonders why her complexion is so bad, why she tires easily, why her digestion is in ruin, and why her head aches.

Woman as a rule do not know how to order a dinner. Men do. I went to an after-theater supper once. There were three women in the party. Here is what they ordered:

No. 1—Lobster salad and ice-cream.

No. 2—Welsh rarebit and a glass of lemonade.

No. 3—Chicken croquettes and a tart.

While at supper they fell to bemoaning the fate of a man who was ruining his system by smoking too much.

Had I dared I should have said:

" My dear ladies, he is not killing himself half so fast as you are. One of you has mixed milk with lobster, a combination nearly as deadly as prussic acid. Another has mingled melted cheese with lemon juice, by way of allaying hunger. A third has prepared her stomach for a night's rest by filling it with fried, greasy, viscid croquettes and rich pastry. What victim to tobacco, or even drink, could do himself worse damage? "

A DAILY PROGRAMME.

But I am wandering from our daily programme.

If you are a woman of leisure, rise at 7 or 7.30. If in business, rise two hours before work begins.

Start the day by standing straight and taking in succession ten long, deep breaths, drawing in and expelling the breath very slowly. Then, keeping the knees rigid, bend forward and try to touch the floor with your fingers. Try this twice the first morning, increasing by one a day till you reach ten times. Move slowly, not with sudden twists of the body.

Do not try the backward bending I advised for men in the last chapter.

Then go through certain motions of the arms (still standing erect, with chest thrown out). Raise the arms straight out at each side, keeping elbows rigid, until the fingers meet over your head. Then bring the arms to the side again and repeat ten times. Then bring the arms up in front until the fingers touch (as in diving position), bringing the arms down again and backward (elbows still rigid) until the fingers meet behind the body. Do each of these ten times.

Then rise twenty times on the toes.

Don't use dumb-bells, Indian clubs, or pulley-weights unless your doctor recommends them. They are, I think, too violent a form of exercise for women.

BATHING AND WALKING.

After these calisthenics take a plunge bath. If your heart is not affected, take a cold bath, into which, the night before, three handfuls of sea salt have been thrown. If you cannot take a cold bath, take one from which the chill has just been removed by a little hot water.

Rub yourself dry with a rough towel.

Eat a breakfast similar to that I recommended, in the last chapter, for men—fruit, cereals, two medium-boiled eggs, toast, and a cup of tea or coffee. Better leave off tea and coffee if you possibly can.

Soon after breakfast (which must NOT be bolted, but which must last at least half an hour), if you are a woman of leisure, take a brisk walk for one mile. If you have to go to work, walk one mile on your way there. People often say: "I live too far uptown to walk to the office."

It never seems to occur to them that they can ride to within a mile of the office, then get off and walk the rest of the way.

If a Brooklynite, walk across the bridge. If a commuter, walk up from the ferry.

When lunch-time comes shut your eyes to the allurements of pie, tart, salad with mayonnaise, fried food, and such-like horrors.

Eat any kind of meat or vegetable you choose, if it

isn't fried.   Take some dessert that is not pastry.   Avoid heavy, cloying foods.

Walk home from work (or one mile of the distance), and if you can get time walk an extra mile, or else try some mild form of athletics.   Go to a women's gymnasium, where the instructor will see that you don't overdo exercise, or else take a spin on your wheel (not a long, tiresome ride nor a "scorch," but an easy jaunt, stopping as soon as you are tired).

AVOID PASTRY.

If you can afford it, ride horseback.   That is still better than cycling.

Join a fencing class, if you can.   Fencing is not only the most beautiful exercise on earth, but one of the most beneficial.   It is also within the physical capabilities of women.

It strengthens the whole body, steadies the nerves, improves the figure, imparts quickness, and does more than any other exercise to make one graceful.

Rest a while before dinner.   Don't eat while exhausted.   Take at least an hour for the meal.

Be careful to eat only such foods as are free from grease and other indigestible properties.   Avoid pastry, fried things, and especially incongruous mixtures. Many foods which, taken separately, are perfectly harmless become murderous taken in combination.

To illustrate: My wife and I dined at a restaurant the evening after my fight with Jeffries. I ordered the meal, which began as follows:

Oysters, cream celery soup, brook trout, etc. I also ordered a bottle of claret.

My wife, while eating her soup, told the waiter to fill her claret glass.

I interposed.

"Better wait till you eat some fish," I said. "If you think cream celery soup and claret go well together just mix cream and vinegar in the same cup some day and watch the result. That is just the combination this soup and claret will form if you take them at the same time."

Yet how many people stop to think of that?

Retire as early after 10 p. m. as possible.

Just before getting into bed drink a glass of ale. Eat a wafer or cracker with it. You will sleep better for this, and it will strengthen your whole system. See that your room is well ventilated.

Women are, as a rule, more nervous than men, and thus require more sleep.

NINE HOURS' SLEEP.

Never spend less than eight hours in bed. Nine is still better—or even ten.

The more sleep a nervous person gets the better. The ale will make you sleep well.

The wholesome diet and steady exercise will benefit the digestion and thus improve your complexion. The exercise, plenty of fresh air, and long sleep will quiet your nerves and add muscle and energy to your body. Your figure will also grow better for the athletic work and good diet.

In other respects follow the hygienic rules I laid down for men in yesterday's lesson.

Keep up this course of treatment steadily.

Avoid late suppers. Choose your food carefully. If you must eat candy and drink ice-cream soda, do so in moderation and soon after meals. NEVER on an empty stomach.

Get an hour's rest in the afternoon if you are a woman of leisure. If you work for your living you can always arrange your leisure hours so as to get time for the exercise I have prescribed.

It costs no more to live healthfully than to live on bad terms with your muscles, nerves, and stomach.

Remember: mild exercise, good diet, lots of fresh air, and plenty of water are Nature's grandest remedies for all ills.

Try my plan for six months.

If you do, you will try it for the rest of your life.

HOW TO BREATHE, STAND, WALK, OR RUN.

By J. Gardner Smith, M. D.

CHAPTER I.

Knowing how to breathe means knowing how to live in perfect health—special training insures strong lungs and develops grace of action.

Dr. J. Gardner Smith, formerly special instructor in physical training in the New York public schools and at present physical director of the Harlem Branch Y. M. C. A, and President of the Harlem Medical Association, has written this series of four articles on the need of outdoor exercise and the best methods to follow to obtain beneficial results in breathing, carriage of the body, walking, and running.

The necessity for outdoor exercise is becoming more appreciated every day. Many instructors, while admitting the good done by gymnasium practice, advise open-air stimulation. How many of the thousands of persons on our streets know how to carry themselves properly?

To economize energy in order to obtain best results with minimum efforts?

To walk properly, to run properly, to stand properly, are natural outcomes of proper breathing. The last helps to aid the others. Without natural breathing the attainment of graceful movement in these exercises is impossible.

Respiratory practice should be begun early in life and continued late. The capacity of the lungs may be thus

Upper chest breathing.

increased. Intelligent breathing does much not only to facilitate walking and running, but to guard against disease.

Bodily demands, of course, depend upon physical exertion. The man who never makes much physical effort may live to a good old age, but he is never prepared for an emergency, such as injury or disease of a portion of the lung, nor can he undergo any violent effort with safety.

CHEST BREATHING.

There are three types of breathing—upper chest, abdominal, and lower chest breathing. An active chest should be always maintained. No effort should be necessary to accomplish this. The muscles should keep it in

Abdominal respiration.

position. In proper respiration the upper chest ought to remain quiet.

Upper chest breathing may be practiced by raising the upper chest upward and forward to the fullest extent. Do not raise the shoulders. Inhale while counting " one, two." Exhale on "three, four." In exhaling the chest should recede and the head should remain erect. Exhale through the nostrils.

In abdominal respiration do not move the chest wall or bend the body. On "one, two," or inhalation, the ab-

Abdominal exhalation.

domen protrudes. At "three, four" it recedes. Press the upper chest with the left hand and place the right palm just below the lower end of the sternum. At every inhalation the right hand should be pushed forward, and on exhalation the abdomen should recede underneath the hand.

The best singers have almost complete control of the lower chest and diaphragm, and breathe little with the upper chest. In lower chest breathing inhale at " one, two," and on " three, four " exhale, distend, and contract the lower chest laterally.

On " one, two " the ribs are rotated outward and raised laterally. Thus the broadest part of the chest is enlarged and much air inhaled. On " three, four," or exhale, expel the air by contracting the lower chest. The upper chest and diaphragm should remain passive. The backs of the fingers or points of index fingers pressing lightly at about the ninth rib will help one to understand this exercise.

A DOZEN A DAY.

In these exercises it is important that there be no constriction about the waist or lower chest. Many women cannot breathe vigorously because of such constriction. Practice in the open air should be sought. Even a dozen deep breaths a day, properly taken, will do much toward strengthening the lungs and getting them in proper condition to bear the strain incidental to walking and running.

The individual who understands how to use his chest is able to meet the strain more readily. In the person who knows how to breathe, shortness of breath is seldom seen.

The effects of proper breathing are better development of and control of the chest muscles, more power in speaking and singing, healthier lung conditions, improved circulation, and better general health.

CHAPTER II.

Dr. J. Gardner Smith has explained how proper breathing insures strength and prolongs life. The good effect on the lungs and voice was pointed out, and the rules governing natural respiration given. To breathe properly one must stand properly. So in this chapter Dr. Smith's hints on how to acquire grace of carriage are published.

HAVING observed the exercises on how to breathe properly, and practiced them gradually and conscientiously, the next step presented is how to stand properly. It is true that these are closely related. To breathe properly one must stand properly. To stand properly one must breathe properly.

The position of the soldier at " Attention ! " gives a clear idea of how to stand properly. He is seen with his heels on the same line and as near each other as the conformation permits. His feet are turned out equally and form with each other an angle of about sixty degrees. The knees are straight without stiffness and the body erect on the hips, inclining a little forward, while the shoulders are square and fall equally. His arms and hands hang naturally, the backs of the hands being turned outward

Correct position for standing.

and the elbows held near the body. The soldier's head is always held erect and squarely to the front, the chin being slightly drawn in, without constraint, while the eyes are straight to the front.

It is essential that the person who would stand properly endeavor at all times to hold the upper chest forward and never assume a stiff attitude.

LACK AMBITION.

Many persons appear with chest sunken and shoulders doubled. They can be seen by hundreds every day. They stand in slouchy attitudes as if they were in danger of falling to pieces. These persons lack life, energy, and ambition. Why? Because they neglect to exercise their

Upper chest exhalation.

lungs. They cannot expect to stand properly if they do not breathe properly.

The reason for the failure to hold the body erect is

traceable to laziness. The muscles of the chest, when
trained by proper respiration, hold that part of the body
in natural position.

The appearance of a West Point cadet before and after
his course at the Military Academy is worthy of notice.
His four years make such a change that his best friends
fail to recognize him. He stands erect. His hands are

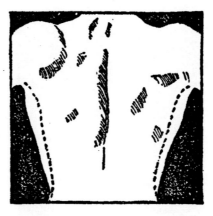

Side action in breathing.

not swinging here, there, and everywhere, neither is he
obliged to put them in his pockets. His elbows are not
pointing at different angles, but hang gracefully near the
body. He does not appear to be stiff-legged, yet his
knees are straight.

His feet do not shift from one position to another, but
are turned out equally and naturally. His body does not
sway this way and that, in embarrassment at not know-

ing how to hold it. It is inclined a little forward, erect on the hips. One shoulder is not higher than the other and constantly shifting. They fall gracefully and equally.

PERFECT REPOSE.

He does not twist his head and neck on to his chin. He looks straight ahead, with chin a little drawn in, and

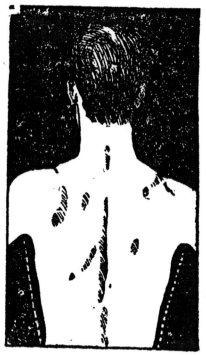

Body in repose.

he holds his upper chest out. As a whole he presents the acme of grace and mobility. He has acquired in standing that most difficult acquirement—repose of manner.

It is not too much to say that knowledge of how to stand properly is an art. Notice the attitudes assumed by persons who pay no attention to this. How awkward and ill at ease they appear when addressing others. They cannot analyze this awkwardness. But a little practice each day in simple exercises, a little thoughtfulness on the subject would do much to obviate the difficulty. All are given the proper facilities. It rests with the individual to improve them.

Proper resting and proper standing are preliminary steps to proper walking and proper running. All are steps toward maintenance of rugged health.

CHAPTER III.

HEEL-AND-TOE ACTION FIRST RULE IN WALKING—NATURAL SWING OF BODY AND FEET GIVES HEALTH AND GRACE OF MOVEMENT—WADDLING IS IMPOSSIBLE WHEN HEAD IS HELD ERECT, CHEST OUT, AND ARMS FOLLOW LEGS—FULL ADVANTAGE TO FAT AND LEAN WHO PRACTICE NOSE BREATHING AND FOLLOW RULES.

To walk correctly is as essential to health as proper breathing. Dr. J. Gardner Smith, who has told how to attain full benefit from natural respiration and the maintenance of the right posture in standing, tells how to carry the body in walking.

WALKING, as practiced by most persons, is neither graceful nor healthful. The fat man puffs and waddles and the thin man goes by jerks. The graceful walker is the exception, but there is no reason why every man and woman should not carry himself or herself as nature intended. Having mastered the proper method of breathing and learned how to stand correctly, walking for health becomes easy.

In walking the heel and toe always strike the ground and at times both feet are on the ground. The graceful

walker springs from the toe at the end of each step or
the beginning of the new step.

The arms should be a little bent at the elbows, chest
out, and head erect.   All breathing should be through the

Both feet on the ground.

nose, never through the mouth.   If a man cannot breathe
through the nose something is wrong with lungs or heart.
In walking no tight clothing should constrict the chest.
The skin ought to be covered with light covering.

A healthful amount of walking depends on individual conditions. The large man can and ought to walk half a mile (ten city blocks) before breakfast at first, and gradually increase this distance to one mile at the end of a month. Superfluous fat will be reduced and he will

Legs like pendulums.

feel better. The thin, nervous man, on the contrary, ought not to walk before eating, as he has no tissue to lose.

In all cases if a person does not walk properly he gains

small benefit from the exercise. The foot is often hampered by narrow shoes, and the spreading action of the toes prevented. The heel first touches and leaves the

Arms follow legs.

ground. The body is alternately supported by first the right and then the left leg.

The legs are like pendulums, and when one leg is put forward and the body assumes an almost vertical position, the other leg is bent, raised, and the body bends forward again. Thus is seen the swinging movement in walking, the bending at the beginning of each step, and the forward inclination and straightening at the end of each step.

In the arms similar movements are noticeable. The right leg and left arm advance simultaneously, as do the left leg and right arm. The leg always swings in the opposite direction to the arm on its own side. When the curves formed by the right and left legs or the right and left arms are joined, they form waved tracks symmetrically arranged on either side of a given line.

The number of steps a person can take in a given time depends on the length of the leg. Everyone has a measure for his steps, which, in walking naturally, he cannot exceed. A tall man will thus take fewer steps in a given time than a short man. In the natural walk all complementary body motions assist.

Many men and women complain that they get out of breath climbing stairs in the city, but they go to the country and climb hills without difficulty. The trouble is that they do not practice walking in town. Women should go upstairs slowly, putting the whole foot on each stair. Climbing stairs is good exercise, and ought to be accomplished without loss of breath.

CHAPTER IV.

ALL MAY RUN WHO LEARN THE RULES OF LEG SPEED—
CATCHING CARS WILL BE A TASK OF JOY AND AN ACT
OF GRACEFUL MOTION—OLD AS WELL AS YOUNG
SHOULD SPRINT AND NONE FEEL THE NEED TO PUFF
AND BLOW—IN RUNNING SPRING FROM THE TOE AND
LET ANKLE, KNEE, AND BODY BEND FREELY.

*In running, if certain natural rules are not observed, in-
jury or, at least, discomfort will result. Dr. J. Gardner Smith points out all of these and tells how young
or old may run and cut a graceful figure.*

RUNNING, which is accelerated walking, presents more
ridiculous spectacles than almost any other exercise. The
man or woman dashing for a car is often a most undig-
nified sight. Such persons expend a needless amount of
nervous and muscular energy in accomplishing something which ought not to even put them out of breath.

Age ought not to interfere with running. An old man
ought not to get out of breath any sooner than a young
one. But there is one thing to be guarded against. That
is heart trouble. All men and women should be exam-
ined, for the victim of heart disease never realizes his

affliction till too late. The lack of pain in initial stages of the disease makes it dangerous.

In running, unlike walking, the heel never strikes the ground, the toe always does. In walking there is a time

Springing from toes.

when both feet are on the ground, in running there is a time when both feet are off the ground. To run gracefully spring from the toe and let ankle, knee, and hip bend freely. The whole body should be in an easy, not a stiff, position.

" When running, no matter what the distance, the arms, or more properly speaking the upper extremities, should be used chiefly from the shoulder, with precision, and should swing in harmony with the legs or lower extremities. The right arm should move with the left leg, and the left arm with the right leg, in order to maintain perfect balance and to gain greater speed. The trunk and head should be allowed to assume their natural position which, if a person carries himself properly, will be in the erect posture or nearly so. The runner ought never to lean forward.

" All distances under and including one mile should be run upon the toes, while distances over one mile should be run upon the ball of the foot, or the part just back of the toes.

" Runners should put their feet out in front of them in a perfectly straight line, making the advanced step with one foot when the other is directly beneath the body, keeping each arm in its relative position and the legs close together, in order to concentrate energy.

" A good stride will cover about 7 feet, 7 feet 2 inches, 7 feet 4 inches, or 7 feet 6 inches. It is a great mistake to overstride, because in so doing an unnecessary amount of energy is wasted, and fatigue comes on more quickly. If one is able to stride 7 feet at first he is doing well. It is best to increase the stride by inches. In this way

a good stride may be obtained without unduly taxing the muscles.

" Never kick your heels up behind you—that is, behind the axis of the body—because it will cause a loss of locomotion and also of time by making the legs trail through a greater space unnecessarily. As one progresses, alighting first upon one set of toes and then upon the other, or ball of the foot, as the case may be, great

care should be exercised in coming down upon the ground lightly. If attention be paid to this the body will escape much jarring, which is important to the muscles and nerves."

The time of a step in quick running, as compared to that in quick walking, is nearly as two to three, while the length of the steps is as two to one. Hence a person can run in a given time three times as fast as he can walk. The velocity in running is usually at a rate of about ten miles an hour.

The correct position at the start.

HOW TO PUNCH THE BAG.

By Gus E. Keeley and Artie R. Keeley, Champion Bag-Punchers of the World.

CHAPTER I.

USEFUL EXERCISE WILL DEVELOP YOUR MUSCLES AND IMPROVE YOUR HEALTH.

This series of lessons in bag-punching shows how your physical condition may be improved, with but little trouble; how at a comparatively small expense you may rig up a bag-punching apparatus in a corner of a small room and how to acquire a knowledge sufficient to make you an expert at the art.

There is no exercise more beneficial to the human system than bag-punching. It is not hard, by any means. Read the lessons, the first of which appears in this chapter, and see the benefits that may be acquired from a regular course of bag-punching.

THE FIRST LESSON.

In the first place, bag-punching is the cheapest, best, most useful exercise in the world.

Do you want to learn to "handle your hands" in a fight—to make yourself strong, quick, and accurate—and to learn how to hit blows that will send the average man to sleep? The punching-bag will teach you all that.

Do you want to become easy and graceful in carriage; to develop each muscle; to improve your health, your figure, and your whole make-up? The punching-bag will do it.

There are other exercises, of course, that will teach you some of these things, but none so effectively and cheaply.

The very cheapness of the exercise commends it. No other good form of calisthenics is half as cheap.

There is a right and wrong way of learning, of course, and we will undertake to teach you the right way.

Let us introduce ourselves. We are the Keeley brothers, champion bag-punchers of the world. We taught ourselves the art, and we are here to teach you.

Follow out our instructions faithfully, and in a few months you will be experts.

THE OUTFIT FIRST.

First of all, let us take up the question of an outfit. Of course, if you are rich and have lots of room at your disposal, there need be no bother about that. But we will suppose, just for the time, that you are not overburdened either with money or space. These lessons are mainly for such people.

If possible, it is well to have a bag that swings from a " platform " or " ceiling." If that is not possible, get

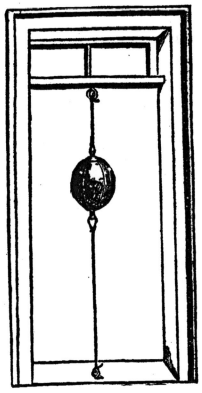

The " double-ender."

a " double-ender " (one that fastens from floor to ceiling).

Such a bag runs in price from ninety-eight cents to two dollars. It has a rubber elastic on one end, a rope on the other. Screws and staples come with it.

Screw one staple into the top of the doorway of your room; the other into the bottom. Do so in such a way as not to prevent the opening or closing of the door.

Fasten the elastic to the top staple and the rope end to the bottom, adjusting them so that the bottom of the bag is at about the height of your throat.

Be sure the rope and rubber are taut, so the bag will have plenty of spring when you hit it.

You can inflate the bag either by blowing into it or with a bicycle pump, which you can buy for twenty-five cents. Have the bag well inflated. It must not be flabby.

THE "PLATFORM" BAG.

Should you get a "platform" you will, of course, only need a "single-end" bag. The "ring platform" is cheapest and best for home use. This consists of a wooden or iron ring, from the center of which the bag hangs. The rope from which the bag is suspended should be long enough to allow the center (or the lower part of the bag, just beneath the center) to touch the ring. Supports come with these "platforms," and they can be screwed up with ease against the wall at whatever height you require.

The ring platforms are better for ring amateur work than the flat "ceilings," and are not nearly so noisy. Hence they are better for home use, especially if the people in the flat below happen to be cranks.

Sash cord is the best, strongest, most durable sort of rope for punching-bags. See that it is renewed as soon

The "platform" bag.

as it shows signs of wear. If you don't, the bag is liable to fly off under some particularly heavy blow and smash something.

COST OF APPARATUS.

The apparatus needed for the "platform" bag is as follows (the prices being put at the lowest possible estimate):

One punching-bag, about, . . .	$1.00
One platform, about, ...	5.00
Sash cord, ...	.25
One pair of striking gloves, . . .	.50
Total cost, ...	$6.75

The striking gloves (a sort of cross between leather mittens and boxing gloves) are used to prevent the hands from becoming sore and to obviate sprains and bruises.

As for costume, wear an old pair of trousers, an undershirt, and a pair of rubber-soled, no-heel shoes. These shoes can be bought for fifty cents a pair.

CHAPTER II.

THESE lessons in bag-punching are intended to show how the physical condition may be improved by this light exercise without a great expense of time or money. The first lesson told how easily the apparatus may be arranged in one's room, the small cost of same, and the costume that might be worn during the exercise. The second lesson in this chapter explains the correct position for the beginner to assume, how to lead properly and strike the first blow, and when to stop.

SECOND LESSON—PROPER POSITION—LEFT- AND RIGHT-
HAND LEADS—GENERAL ADVICE.

Now that you have your apparatus and costume ready, let us begin our first lesson.

When you take up your first position, stand much as you would if you were sparring—that is, stand with the left foot about eighteen inches in front of the right, the toes of each foot turned slightly outward, the right toe being turned out farther than the left, the balance being kept perfect.

Keep the knees unbent.

Hold shoulders slightly back and head erect. Keep the right hand (when not hitting with it) across the wind and slightly in advance of the body. Let the left arm be half extended, the elbow a little forward of the hip, the forearm straight ahead.

Don't stand too close to the bag. If you do it may cramp your motions, and besides you are more apt to hurt your face. Do not, on the other hand, stand so far away from the bag that your elbow will not easily touch it when the bag is not in motion.

HOW TO STRIKE THE FIRST BLOW.

Now for the first blow.

Hit out straight from the shoulder with your left hand, striking the ball as near the center (between top and bottom) as possible, and throwing the weight of the left shoulder and the upper part of the body into the blow. The bag will hit the ring of the platform and rebound. Be careful that it does not hit your face in doing so. Either move the face to the right to avoid it or else step back out of reach.

The bag will, of course, fly off at wrong angles at first, for it is not as easy as it looks to hit it in just the right

way to insure its striking the ring and returning to you just where you expect it. But a very little practice will teach you the knack.

The bag, as we said, will hit the ring, fly back to the opposite side, and again strike the side it hit first, swinging once more toward you.

As it returns this second time, hit it again with the left, making it go through the same evolutions as before, and, as it comes back the second time, repeat the blow.

Keep this up until you can do it fairly well and can judge as to the strength of the blow necessary.

THE RIGHT LEAD.

When you have mastered this (it isn't quite as easy as it sounds, just at first) lead with the right instead of the left, making the bag go through the same evolutions as before, only using the right hand instead of the left.

When you have mastered this, try it with alternate hands. Hit it with the left, let it strike the ring in front of you (then the opposite side of the ring and the first spot again); then, as it comes back, hit it with the right and let it swing as before.

Get so you can hit it with precision with alternate hands without missing, without losing your balance, or getting rattled.

These are the first and fundamental motions of bag-punching. Until you learn them thoroughly you can never master the rest.

Take great care to hit the bag square; not with a twisting or downward or upward blow. Such blows spoil accuracy, weaken hitting powers, and may sprain the arm.

WHEN TO STOP.

Never punch the bag after it begins to tire you. As soon as you get tired rest. Punch it at first for three minutes steadily. Then rest. Then, when rested, try three more minutes of punching. Only as soon as you become really fatigued be sure to stop for the day. Increase the time of punching little by little as you find you can stand it.

We have gotten so now that we can punch it for over an hour without tiring at all.

CHAPTER III.

TATTOO AND HOOK BLOWS FOR THE BAG-PUNCHER—
HOW TO BECOME PROFICIENT IN THE ART OF LANDING
BLOWS QUICKLY AND CORRECTLY, EXPLAINED BY THE
CHAMPION KEELEY BROTHERS.

THAT bag-punching is a most beneficial exercise there
is no doubt, and these lessons should make it easier for
a beginner.

The first lesson told how easily the apparatus may be
arranged in one's room, the small cost of same, and the
costume that might be worn during the exercise. The
second lesson explains the correct position for the beginner to assume, how to lead properly and strike the
first blow, and when to stop. In this chapter the tattoo,
swings, and half-hooks are explained.

Now that you have learned to hit the bag on the third
rebound with alternate hands, try the next step.

Stand as before. Lead with the left for the bag, hitting it with just enough force to drive it against the ring
and back against your fist. Don't let it rebound to the
opposite side of the ring this time, but hit it as it comes
back from its first contact with the ring, and drive it
back again, repeating this process until you have gauged

the force and direction of the blow correctly and have learned to hit the bag rapidly this way.

Then go through the same motions with the right hand, until fairly proficient.

When you have mastered the trick with each hand, try both.

Hit the bag with the left fist, driving it against the ring. As it bounds back hit it with the right and so on as long as possible.

You cannot do this quickly at first, but in a very few days you can do it with lightning speed, making the ball rattle continuously against the ring like a roll of a drum beating the tattoo.

THE "TATTOO" PUNCH.

This motion is known among bag-punchers as the "tattoo," because of its resemblance to the roll of a drum.

Practice it in this way until proficient.

Then try the tattoo with the hands over-lapping, in much the same motion as if rolling up a ball of twine on the hands. You can reach great speed this way. Be sure, however, not to let the hands hit or brush against each other while doing this tattoo. The two different modes of working the tattoo, described above, bring out different muscles.

Now stand in position again. Drop the left arm to

the side. Bring it around in a semicircle, throwing the shoulder with it, keeping the arm almost rigid and turning the forearm so that the back of the knuckles will

Straight tattoo.

strike the bag. This is a left-arm swing and can be delivered with terrific force.

Do the same with the right. Then alternately, allowing the bag to hit the sides of the ring three or perhaps four times between your blows.

Judging direction and distance in such a move is not as easy as you may think. Much depends on hitting the bag at the proper angle and at the proper time. It should be hit as it is swinging toward you and while it is as nearly in the center of the ring as possible.

SOME LEFT HOOKS.

Next we'll try some half-hooks.

Bend the left arm at an angle of almost ninety degrees. Then drop the fist to the level of the thigh and bring the

Overhand tattoo.

arm around with the same motion as in a swing (not, however, turning the hand as in the swing), and throw your shoulder with the blow. Hit the bag square, not slantingly nor in such fashion as to throw it out of line.

Hit it so it will strike the ring and rebound straight, as usual. Most of the effectiveness of a half-hook depends on the quickness and accuracy with which it is delivered

Left-hand half hook.

and the weight of shoulder and body that is thrown into the blow.

Next try right-hand half-hooks, and then alternate from left to right and right to left.

In striking these heavy blows great care must be taken not to stand too close to the bag or to let it hit you on the rebound. Learn to judge by experience the distance at which you can best land such blows.

TO AVOID THE BAG.

As for avoiding the rebound of the bag, a good way to learn that is to lead a straight left-hand blow (not too

hard) at close quarters, then duck the bag as it comes
back or else shift the head and shoulders to right or to
left so as to avoid it.   This is easily learned and will

Right-hand half hook.

prove of the greatest value to you in avoiding the blows
of a real adversary.

Indeed, the swings and half-hooks we have taught you
are among the deadliest blows used by pugilists.

While it is well to keep out of fights, yet it is also well
to learn how to strike a good blow in case you are ever
forced into one.   This is one of the grand advantages of
the punching-bag.

CHAPTER IV.

HOW TO BECOME FANCY IN PUNCHING THE BAG—RIGHT AND LEFT ELBOW BLOWS AND A NEW AND PRETTY TATTOO.

THE first lesson told how easily the apparatus may be arranged in one's room, the small cost of same, and the costume that might be worn during the exercise. The second lesson explained the correct position for the beginner to assume, how to lead properly and strike the first blow, and when to stop. In the last chapter the tattoo, swings, and half-hooks were explained. Elbow blows and elbow tattoos are the subjects in this chapter.

Now let us come to elbow work.

This is hard and awkward, just at first, but if you work at it faithfully you will soon get the hang of it. When you do, the thing will be very easy.

A good deal depends on proper balance. Your own instinct and a little practice will soon teach you this, just as it taught you to judge distance in hitting.

One point more before we come down to our next lesson: A lot of fellows when they find they can't pick up the whole science of bag-punching in a week, get discouraged and quit. It is not to such men that we are talking. The chances are ten to one that they will never make a success of anything in life, having so little perseverance. But there is another class—men who lose their tempers ("get mad," to use a schoolboy term) when the bag does not behave just as they expect it to. They either stop then, or hammer the bag angrily and wildly, spoiling any good effect the exercise might bring.

MUST HAVE PATIENCE.

Such men must remember the fault is not with the bag, but with their own awkwardness. Nothing but patience and perseverance will overcome the difficulty.

As a "temper-improver" the punching-bag is a winner.

Now for the elbow work. Stand in position, throw the left arm out, the arm from shoulder to elbow being almost parallel with the shoulder, the arm from elbow to wrist being bent at right angles to the rest of the arm.

By turning the left arm and shoulder hit the bag with the elbow, driving the bag against the ring, letting it rebound to the other side of the ring and back again, and hitting it with the elbow once more on the third rebound. The blow is not nearly as easy to do accurately as when delivered with the fist, for the simple reason that you are not accustomed to use the elbow for that purpose, and are inclined to be awkward at it just at first. But practice will soon make you familiar with it.

RIGHT ELBOW BLOW.

Let the right side of the left elbow (when forearm is turned downward) hit the bag. When hitting a " back

Forward elbow blow.

elbow blow " (which will come later) hit with the other side of the elbow. For the sake of convenience we will call the present elbow blow (and all elbow blows that drive the bag in front of you rather than behind) " forward elbow blows."

After learning the forward elbow blow with the left arm, try it with the right.

In the right-arm work keep the left foot still advanced, but turn the right shoulder further forward so that the

Right fist and elbow tattoo.

chest is flush with the bag, and at the necessary distance from it.   You will soon learn the distance as well as the required balance and motion for hips and shoulders.

After learning to hit the bag with the elbow on the third rebound try it on the first rebound.

After that hit it with the left elbow and on the third rebound hit it with the right, alternating. Then with left and right on first rebound as in tattoo.

A NEW TATTOO.

Next we will try a new and pretty tattoo, which is really not so very hard:

Back elbow blow.

Hit the bag with the left elbow. On the rebound hit it with the right fist. Let it strike the ring, and as it comes back hit it again with the left elbow, driving it against the ring and tapping it once more with the right fist as it comes back, keeping this up as long as you can. You will in time learn to do it almost as quickly as you can now work the regular fist tattoo. No shift of shoulders and chest is necessary when working from left elbow to right fist in this tattoo.

After mastering this try the same thing with right elbow and left fist.

Now we'll practice some back elbow blows.

Hold the left arm as when dealing a forward elbow blow; but hit the bag with the opposite side of the elbow. This will drive it to the ring somewhat behind you, making it more difficult to hit it again on the third or even the first rebound. Practice it faithfully, going slow at first, and in time you can acquire it.

Then try it with the right elbow in the same way.

This lesson has been anything but easy. Still it is important, and can be learned with a little patience. In the next chapter we will go still further into fancy work.

CHAPTER V.

HITTING BAG WITH HEAD STRENGTHENS THE NECK.

HEAD blows, double, triple, and quadruple rolls are explained in this lesson in bag-punching.

The first lesson told how easily the apparatus may be arranged in one's room, the small cost of same, and the costume that might be worn during the exercise. The second lesson explained the correct position for the beginner to assume, how to lead properly and strike the first blow, and when to stop. Next the tattoo, swings, and half-hooks were explained. Elbow blows and elbow tattoos were the subjects of the last lesson.

Having mastered the single back elbow blows, try a variation or two on them: Stand with your back to the bag, being careful to judge the proper distance. Hit a back blow with the left elbow, and on the first rebound hit the bag a back blow with the right elbow, keeping up the motion in a sort of tattoo. This is very hard. Great care and patience must be used in striking the bag so as to make it rebound in such a way as to bring it in reach of the other elbow. When you have learned this thoroughly try another move, which you are to use later in conjunction with this back elbow tattoo.

Stand with the back to the bag. Bend backward slightly so as to hit the bag with the back of the head. Do not butt it hard; only hard enough to make it hit the

One of the head blows.

ring and rebound. As it rebounds butt it once more with the back of the head. This is not hard, the direction and necessary force being soon acquired. Do not bend too far back for this, so as to lose the balance.

The movement looks ridiculous, but it is not. It not only strengthens the muscles of the neck, but it is an important part of an intricate maneuver which we will now come to.

Stand with the back to the bag as before. Hit the

Right elbow punch.

bag lightly with the left elbow, so that on the rebound it will hit the head.

Butt it back against the ring with the head, giving it

a slight tendency to the right, and on the rebound hit it with the right elbow, knocking it to the left, so that it will hit the head on the rebound.

The left elbow blow.

With the head butt it so that it will rebound to the left elbow.

Repeat as before in the following order:

Left elbow, head, right elbow; right elbow, head, left elbow.

You will easily get the hang of this intricate and seem

ingly difficult motion when once you have mastered the elbow blows from behind, described in the first part of this chapter.

This head and elbow motion is known as the "triple back roll."

Now turn around and face the bag once more, standing as in other lessons.

Hit the bag a "forward elbow blow" with the left elbow. Let it strike the ring; and on the first rebound hit it with the left fist. Let it hit the ring and on the first rebound hit it with the left elbow again, working thus a sort of one-arm tattoo.

Then do the same with the right elbow and fist.

Having mastered both of these, try the following combination of the two:

Hit the bag with the left elbow, let it rebound. Then hit it (on first rebound) with the left fist. Then on the first rebound hit it with the right fist. On the first rebound hit it with the right elbow. On the first rebound, then, hit it with the right fist. So on to the left fist and left elbow in the same fashion and back again.

This is soon learned and is a very pretty maneuver. It is called the "quadruple roll."

The "triple roll" is still easier and is merely a simpler form of the "quadruple." To work it, hit the bag with the left elbow. On the first rebound hit it with the left fist. On first rebound hit it with right fist, then with left elbow, left fist, and right fist again. The same

" triple roll " may be worked from the right (that is: right elbow, right fist, left fist).

Next try the head blow from in front, just as you learned it from the rear. It will be useful in a new maneuver explained in the next chapter.

CHAPTER VI.

ROLL BLOWS AND TRAINING POINTERS FOR BAG-PUNCHERS.

THE Keeley brothers, the champion bag-punchers of the world, complete their lessons in bag-punching in this chapter with the circular roll and training suggestions as the subjects.

The first lesson told how easily the apparatus may be arranged in one's room, the small cost of same, and the costume that might be worn during the exercise. The second lesson explained the correct position for the beginner to assume, how to lead properly and strike the first blow, and when to stop. Next the tattoo, swings, and half-hooks were explained. Elbow blows and elbow tattoos, head blows, double, triple, and quadruple rolls have also been explained.

Now we come to an intricate and pretty maneuver that combines all the moves taught in the fifth lesson.

Stand facing the bag. Hit it with the left fist; hit with the front of the head on the first rebound, and then with the right fist, and so on to the right elbow. Thus far the maneuver is simply the quadruple roll and the head blow. But this is only part of it.

After hitting the bag a forward blow with the right elbow let it rebound twice, catching it a back elbow blow with the right elbow on the second rebound.

Circular roll, first blow.

Let the bag rebound once from this blow, hitting it with the back of the head on the first rebound. Then a back elbow blow with the left elbow, letting it rebound twice and catching it a forward elbow blow with the left elbow on the second rebound, thus completing the circle.

Start it along as before.

Hard as this sounds, it is really easy if you have mastered the various moves that go to make it up.

It is a maneuver that brings almost every muscle of the body into play, and requires a quick eye and a cool brain.

The motions requiring circular evolutions of the bag can, of course, only be used on " platform " punching-bags, as the " double-enders " are not capable of such movements.

With double-ender bags you may use all the blows of a pugilist, however, and they are as good for developing your hitting powers, balance, and reach as are the platform bags.

The double-ender bag may be rigged up in the doorway of even the smallest hall bedroom. It won't interfere with the opening and closing of the door, and can be taken down or put up in less than one minute.

You can use straight leads, hooks, swings, and even upper-cuts on it, and can work the tattoo as well, either with both hands or with fist and elbow.

We would suggest the following course of mild training:

Sleep at least eight hours. Rise at seven. Before dressing, punch the bag briskly for three minutes—don't punch it too long or too hard at that time; it is bad for you to become overtired before breakfast. Then bathe in a tub, or, if this is not convenient, take a cold sponge bath, rubbing yourself hard with a rough towel. Dress,

Circular roll, halfway round.

and, if you have time, walk briskly for five or six blocks (not too far) before breakfast.

You'll come in hungry, but don't overeat, and, above all, don't bolt your food.

When possible take most of your punching-bag exercise in afternoon or evening rather than in the forenoon. Punch the bag until you are tired and then stop for the day. Either punch it, not too violently, for fifteen minutes, or else for a few hard three-minute rounds, taking one minute's rest between rounds.

As for diet, avoid too many sweets, pastry, and starchy foods, if you wish to keep your weight down. Eat heartily, and learn by experience what sort of food best agrees with you. Keep your digestion good; don't sit up late. Steer clear of drink and tobacco. Nothing else so soon queers the nerves and breaks up the constitution.

Inside of three months you can become fairly proficient at bag-punching. From that time on you will steadily improve for about two years, until you reach the limit of proficiency.